LAMDA
ANTHOLOGY OF VERSE AND PROSE

LAMDA
ANTHOLOGY OF VERSE AND PROSE
VOLUME XVI

Introduction by Roger McGough

PUBLISHED BY
OBERON BOOKS
FOR THE LONDON ACADEMY OF
MUSIC AND DRAMATIC ART

This edition first published in 2003 for LAMDA Ltd.
by Oberon Books Ltd.
(incorporating Absolute Classics)
521 Caledonian Road, London N7 9RH
Tel: 0171 607 3637 / Fax: 0171 607 3629
e-mail: oberon.books@btinternet.com
www.oberonbooks.com

A catalogue record for this book is available from the British Library.

ISBN 1 84002 397 X

Cover design: Joe Ewart

Printed in Great Britain by Antony Rowe Ltd, Chippenham.

Contents

Introduction

Having written a five-thousand word introduction about the power of the human voice, the delight in reciting verse and prose, and the importance of public-speaking examinations, I realised that I would be telling the reader nothing that he, or she, did not already know. (Except perhaps, for my light-hearted recollections of the Waterloo and Crosby Festival of Music and Drama in 1949, when I recited 'Jabberwocky' to great acclaim and earned my Elementary (Grade One) Certificate in Speech and Drama. (*'This certificate not to be used as a teaching qualification'*). Instead, using a pair of golden scissors, I cut up poems taken from this LAMDA Anthology of Verse and Prose and composed the following...

Let us celebrate the speaking of verse and prose
The fellowship of the nightingale and the rose

Your nose itches, your palms perspire
All the world's a stage, O for a muse of fire

For if music and sweet poetry agree
Walk in the wolfwood, journey to the River Sea

Sing of alarm clocks covered in fur
The aching eyes of an old dancing bear

Of breaches, ambuscados, Spanish blades
How the great gales rage and the applemoon fades

Songs of mischievous dogs and the tug of war
Like as the waves make towards the pebbled shore

A swirling whirling dragon weaving to and fro
Will time say nothing but I told you so?

For in my heart there stirs a quiet pain
Twitching to each subtle electric flutter of the brain

I who have flowed through history
Going barefoot and constantly risking absurdity

Let us rejoice in the communion of souls
Grace notes for hard times, the way her smile unfolds

Let us celebrate the spoken word, and your timeless voice
Tip-toeing on consonants, sliding along vowels. Rejoice.

Roger McGough

INTRODUCTORY

THE STORM

In my bed all safe and warm
I like to listen to the storm.
The thunder rumbles loud and grand –
The rain goes splash and whisper: and
The lightning is so sharp and bright
It sticks its fingers through the night.

Dorothy Aldis

WATER EVERYWHERE

There's water on the ceiling,
And water on the wall,
There's water in the bedroom,
And water in the hall,
There's water on the landing,
And water on the stair,
Whenever Daddy takes a bath
There's water everywhere.

Valerie Bloom

HIPPOPOTAMUS

The hippopotamus –
how odd –
loves rolling
in the river mud.

It makes him
neither hale nor ruddy,
just lovely
hippopotamuddy.

N M Bodecker

CAT KISSES

Sandpaper kisses
on a cheek or a chin –
that is the way
for a day to begin!

Sandpaper kisses –
a cuddle, a purr.
I have an alarm clock
that's covered with fur.

Bobbi Katz

TWO FUNNY MEN

I know a man
Who's upside down,
And when he goes to bed
His head's not on the pillow. No!
His *feet* are there instead.

I know a man
Who's back to front,
The strangest man *I've* seen.
He can't tell where he's going
But he knows where he has been.

Spike Milligan

TO THE FAIR

When Dad and I went to the fair
we tried out all of the rides,
we dodged about on the dodgems
and whizzed down the astro slide.
Then we rode the roller coaster
and it gave us quite a scare:
'One thing is certain,' Dad said,
'I'm not going back on there!'

Brian Moses

GROUP INTRODUCTORY

ELEPHANT WALKING

We're swaying through the jungle
Dizzy with the heat,
Searching for a water-hole
To cool our heavy feet.

Trample on the grasses;
Then stop and breathe the scent
Of flower and leaf—and tiger!
And we watch the way he went.

Then on again we stumble,
Searching for a drink;
We find a spilling river,
And into it we sink.

Clive Sansom

BURIED TREASURE

I went into the garden.
I dug down in the ground
To look for buried treasure
And this is what I found:

Crawly things
Creepy things
Things with shiny tails
Centipedes
Millepedes
Snails snails snails

Creepy things
Crawly things
Little beady bugs
Millepedes
Centipedes
Slugs slugs slugs.

Richard James

SEA SHORE

Sandy shore and sea-weed;
Rocks and cockle-shells;
Pebbles round and salty;
Dead fish smells.

Sun on bending water;
Donkeys jingling bells;
Hoofprints in sand-ripples;
Salt-water wells.

Boats against the sunshine;
Seagulls' squealing hells;
Spray on brown faces;
Small boys' yells.

John Kitching

PREPARATORY

THE SCHOOL PLAY

I'm in the school play this Christmas,
I've got an important part;
So I'm learning and learning and learning my lines
Until I can say them by heart.

When I go on stage I'll be nervous,
I'm sure I'll forget what to say.
You see I'm the front of the pantomime horse –
"Neigh, neigh, neigh, neigh, NEIGH!"

Georgie Adams

MY GRANNIES

I hate it, in the holiday,
When Grandma brings her pets to stay –
Her goat, her pig, her seven rats
Scare our dog and chase our cats.
Her budgies bite, her parrots shout –
And guess who has to clean them out?

My other Gran, the one I like,
Always brings her motor-bike,
And when she takes me for a ride
To picnic in the countryside,
We zoom up hills and whizz round bends –
I hate it when her visit ends!

June Crebbin

THE LONELY DRAGON

A dragon is sad
Because everyone thinks
A dragon is fierce and brave,
And roars out flames,
And eats everybody,
Whoever comes near his cave.
But a dragon likes people,
A dragon needs friends,
A dragon is lonely and sad,
If anyone knows
Of a friend for a dragon,
A dragon would be very glad.   ·

Theresa Heine

TEN THINGS FOUND
IN A WIZARD'S POCKET

A dark night.
Some words that nobody could ever spell.
A glass of water full to the top.
A large elephant.
A vest made from spiders' webs.
A handkerchief the size of a car park.
A bill from the wand shop.
A bucket full of stars and planets, to mix with the dark night.
A bag of magic mints you can suck for ever.
A snoring rabbit.

Ian McMillan

KNIGHT-IN-ARMOUR

Whenever I'm a shining Knight,
I buckle on my armour tight;
And then I look about for things,
Like Rushings-out, and Rescuings,
And Savings from the Dragon's Lair,
And fighting all the Dragons there.
And sometimes when our fights begin,
I think I'll let the Dragons win...
And then I think perhaps I won't,
Because they're Dragons, and I don't.

A A Milne

EXPERIMENT

at school we're doing growing things
    with cress.
sprinkly seeds in plastic pots
    of cotton wool.

Kate's cress sits up on the sill
    she gives it water.
mine is shut inside the cupboard
    dark and dry.

now her pot has great big clumps
    of green
mine hasn't.
Mrs Martin calls it Science
    I call it mean.

Danielle Sensier

GROUP PREPARATORY

WIND POEM

Wind slices its icy blade.

Wind raids trees,
smacks leaves up back streets.

Wind somersaults sheets,
bustles and kicks.

Wind flexes muscles,
flicks its quivering wrist.

Wind twists dustbins
into clattering cartwheels.

Wind curls its steel tongue
like a shout flung at the sky.

Wind sighs;
Dies.

Pie Corbett

IT IS I, THE LITTLE OWL

Who is it up there on top of the lodge?
Who is it up there on top of the lodge?
    It is I,
    The little owl,
    coming down –
    It is I,
    The little owl,
    coming down –
    coming down –
    down –
    coming
    down –
    down –

Who is it whose eyes are shining up there?
Who is it whose eyes are shining up there?
    It is I,
    The little owl,
    coming down –
    It is I,
    The little owl,
    coming down –
    coming –
    down –
    coming
    down –
    down –

Chippewa Indian

BUSY DAY

Pop in
pop out
pop over the road
pop out for a walk
pop in for a talk
pop down to the shop
can't stop
got to pop

got to pop?

pop where?
pop what?

well
I've got to
pop round

pop up
pop in to town
pop out to see
pop in for tea
pop down to the shop
can't stop
got to pop

got to pop?

pop where?
pop what?

well
I've got to
pop in
pop out
pop over the road
pop out for a walk
pop in for a talk...

Michael Rosen

PRELIMINARY

A SMILE

Smiling is infectious,
You catch it like the flu.
When someone smiled at me today
I started smiling too.

I passed around the corner
And someone saw my grin.
When he smiled, I realised
I'd passed it on to him.

I thought about my smile and then
I realised its worth.
A single smile like mine could travel
Right around the earth.

If you feel a smile begin
Don't leave it undetected.
Let's start an epidemic quick
And get the world infected.

Jez Alborough

HOUSE

The ruins of an old house stand
Without a roof, on muddy land,
Each window is a sightless eye
Staring at the city sky.

Locks are broken, every wall
Looks as if about to fall.
The people who lived here, they say,
Just packed up and went away.

And once when I was playing there
Halfway up the curving stair
I thought I heard a laughing sound
Coming from the trampled ground.

Leonard Clark

AN ALIEN EDUCATION

Miss Jones has been kidnapped
by an alien creature,
who hadn't realised
that she was our teacher.

But it's not so unusual,
it's an easy mistake,
it's the sort of error
anyone could make.

Just ask any alien
in the kidnapping game,
for teachers and aliens –
well, they all look the same!

Andrew Collett

CHIPS

Out of the paper bag
Comes the hot breath of the chips
And I shall blow on them
To stop them burning my lips.

Before I leave the counter
The woman shakes
Raindrops of vinegar on them
And salty snowflakes.

Outside the frosty pavements
Are slippery as a slide
But the chips and I
Are warm inside.

Stanley Cook

WORDS THAT DESCRIBE THE EATING HABITS OF TWO DINOSAURS AND MY COUSIN

Carnivorous means that you eat only meat
Like the gigantic fearsome *T. rex*.
Herbivorous means that you eat only plants
Like the brachiosaurs with long necks.
But I've got a word to describe Cousin Pete
Whose strange eating habits arise –
Frenchfrivorous tells you about what he'll eat,
Since all that he eats is french fries.

Jeff Moss

FLYING

I saw the moon
One windy night,
Flying so fast –
All silvery white –
Over the sky,
Like a toy balloon
Loose from its string –
A runaway moon.
The frosty stars
Went racing past,

Chasing her on
Ever so fast.
Then everyone said,
'It's the clouds that fly,
And the stars and moon
Stand still in the sky.'
But I don't mind –
I saw the moon
Sailing away
Like a toy
Balloon.

J M Westrup

GROUP PRELIMINARY

HIST WHIST

hist   whist
little ghostthings
tip-toe
twinkle-toe

little twitchy
witches and tingling
goblins
hob-a-nob   hob-a-nob

little hoppy happy
toad in tweeds
tweeds
little itchy mousies

with scuttling
eyes   rustle and run   and
hidehidehide
whisk

whisk   look out for the old woman
with the wart on her nose
what she'll do to yer
nobody knows

for she knows the devil   ooch
the devil   ouch
the devil
ach   the great

green
dancing
devil
devil

devil
devil

        wheeEEE

E E Cummings

CAT!

Cat!
Scat!
Atter her, atter her,
Sleeky flatterer,
Spitfire chatterer,
Scatter her, scatter her
  Off her mat!
  Wuff!
  Wuff!
  Treat her rough!
Git her, git her,
Whiskery spitter!
Catch her, catch her,
Green-eyed scratcher!
  Slathery
  Slithery
  Hisser,
  Don't miss her!
Run till you're dithery,
  Hithery
  Thithery
  Pfitts! pfitts!
  How she spits!
  Spitch! Spatch!
  Can't she scratch!
Scritching the bark
Of the sycamore-tree,
She's reached her ark
And's hissing at me

Pfitts! pfitts!
Wuff! wuff!
    Scat,
    Cat!
    That's
    That!

Eleanor Farjeon

CHINESE NEW YEAR DRAGON

There's a brightly coloured dragon
Swaying down the street,
Stomping and stamping
And kicking up its feet.

There's a multi-coloured dragon
—Green, gold, and red—
Twisting and twirling
And shaking its head.

There's a silky-scaled dragon
Parading through the town,
Swishing and swooshing
And rippling up and down.

There's a swirling, whirling dragon,
Weaving to and fro,
Prancing and dancing
And putting on a show.

There's cheering and clapping
As the dragon draws near—
A sign of good luck
And a happy New Year!

John Foster

ENTRY

HE WAS A RAT

He was a rat, and she was a rat,
        And down in one hole they did dwell,
And both were as black as a witch's cat,
        And they loved each other well.

He had a tail, and she had a tail,
        Both long and curling and fine;
And each said, 'Yours is the finest tail
        In the world, excepting mine.'

He smelt the cheese, and she smelt the cheese,
        And they both pronounced it good;
And both remarked it would greatly add
        To the charms of their daily food.

So he ventured out, and she ventured out,
        And I saw them go with pain;
But what befell them I never can tell,
        For they never came back again.

                    Anon.

HAIR

I despair
About hair
        With all the fuss
        For us
Of snipping
And clipping
        Of curling
        And twirling,
Of tying
And drying,

And lopping
And flopping,
And flurries
And worries,
About strength,
The length,
As it nears
The ears
Or shoulder.
When you're older
It turns grey
Or goes away
Or leaves a fuzz
Hair does!

Max Fatchen

SOARFISH THE SWORDFISH

The swordfish saws
through the grain
of each wave

Storing the off-cuts
in his
decorative cave

There he sands
wooden knick-knacks
he's carved for himself

Which he proudly
displays on a
waterproof shelf

He chisels
and whittles and
varnishes things

Like wardrobes
and mountains and
oak angel wings

If you walk
on a beach
with no driftwood around

And you're slightly
aware of a
faint, grating sound

Put your ear
to the ocean
and you'll hear I suppose

The tone of
the swordfish
sharpening his nose.

Stewart Henderson

BROTHER

I had a little brother
And I brought him to my mother
And I said I want another
Little brother for a change.
But she said don't be a bother
So I took him to my father
And said this little bother
Of a brother's very strange.

But he said one little brother
Is exactly like another
And every little brother
Misbehaves a bit he said.
So I took the little bother
From my mother and my father
And put the little bother
Of a brother back to bed.

Mary Ann Hoberman

NEW BOOK

As you open its lid your mind unlocks.
The book itself is a brand new box.
And you pore that book by day and night,
For the book is a block of pure delight.
Then when you've done and the text is read
and your eyes are tired but your mind feels fed,
you may place that book on the silent shelf
but a bit of the book has become your new self.

Tony Mitton

IF PIGS COULD FLY

If pigs could fly, I'd fly a pig
To foreign countries small and big –
To Italy and Spain,
To Austria, where cowbells ring,
To Germany, where people sing –
And then come home again.

I'd see the Ganges and the Nile;
I'd visit Madagascar's isle,
And Persia and Peru.
People would say they'd never seen
So odd, so strange an air-machine
As that on which I flew.

Why, everyone would raise a shout
To see his trotters and his snout
Come floating from the sky;
And I would be a famous star
Well known in countries near and far –
If only pigs could fly!

James Reeves

GOING BAREFOOT

With shoes on,
I can only feel
how hard or soft
the rock or sand is
where I walk
or stand.

Barefoot,
I can feel
how warm mud
moulds my soles—
or how cold
pebbles
knead them
like worn knuckles.

Curling my toes,
I can drop
an anchor
to the sea floor—
hold fast
to the shore
when the tide
tows.

Judith Thurman

SHADOWS

Moon
Last evening you
Rolled so loud and silver
Past my window
That the shadows
Woke and wove their dark
Molasses stripes
Over my bed

And
In the criss-cross of
That night-time
I knew what to do
Breathe soft
Breathe soft
And fold into a quiet silhouette
Until morning

Zaro Weil

GRADE ONE

THE NIGHT IS DARKENING ROUND ME

The night is darkening round me,
The wild winds coldly blow;
But a tyrant spell has bound me
And I cannot, cannot go.

The giant trees are bending
Their bare boughs weighed with snow,
The storm is fast descending
And yet I cannot go.

Clouds beyond clouds above me,
Wastes beyond wastes below;
But nothing drear can move me;
I will not, cannot go.

Emily Bronte

I THINK MY TEACHER IS A COWBOY

It's not just
That she rides to school on a horse
And carries a Colt 45 in her handbag.

It's not just
the way she walks;
hands hanging over her hips.

It's not just
the way she dresses;
stetson hat and spurs on her boots.

It's not just the way she talks;
calling the playground the corral,
the Head's room the Sheriff's office,
the school canteen the chuck wagon,

the school bus the stagecoach,
the bike sheds the livery stable.

What gives her away
Is when the hometime pips go.
She slaps her thigh
And cries
'Yee ha!'

John Coldwell

MONSTER

I saw a monster in the woods
As I was cycling by,
His footsteps smouldered in the leaves,
His breath made bushes die,

And when he raised his hairy arm
It blotted out the sun;
He snatched a pigeon from the sky
And swallowed it in one.

His mouth was like a dripping cave,
His eyes like pools of lead,
And when he growled I rode back home
And rushed upstairs to bed.

But that was yesterday and though
It gave me quite a fright,
I'm older now and braver so
I'm going back tonight.

I'll tie him up when he's asleep
And take him to the zoo.
The trouble is he's rather big…
Will you come too?

Richard Edwards

FRIENDS

I fear it's very wrong of me,
And yet I must admit,
When someone offers friendship
I want the *whole* of it.
I don't want everybody else
To share my friends with me.
At least, I want *one* special one,
Who, indisputably,

Likes me much more than all the rest,
Who's always on my side,
Who never cares what others say,
Who lets me come and hide
Within his shadow, in his house –
It doesn't matter where –
Who lets me simply be myself,
Who's always, *always* there.

Elizabeth Jennings

THE BOY WHO DROPPED LITTER

'ANTHONY WRIGGLY
SHAME ON YOU!'
screeched the teacher
as she spotted him
scrunching up his crisp packet
and dropping it carefully
on to the pavement outside school.

'If everyone went around
dropping crisp packets like you do
where would we be?'

(Anthony didn't know, so she told him)

'We'd be wading waist-high in crisp packets,
that's where!'

Anthony was silent.
He hung his head.

It looked to the teacher
as if he was very sorry.

When in fact he was trying to calculate
just how many packets it would take
to bring Basildon to a complete standstill.

Lindsay MacRae

READING TIME

Please, Mrs Harris.
There's a bat
on the mat....

Well read, Sue,
but, right just now
I'm listening to....

No, Mrs Harris,
I mean
There IS a bat
on the mat!

Oh, a bat and ball!
Thank you, Sue,
Just pick it up
and pop it in the hall
for PE time, can you?

NO, Mrs Harris,
I mean a BAT,
Just like I said.

I think it might be dead.
Shall I bring it here,
or will you come and....

OH, Mrs Harris, LOOK!
It ISN'T dead.
Can you see its furry head?
I think it's waking up!
Mrs Harris.....?

Judith Nicholls

I AM FALLING OFF A MOUNTAIN

I am falling off a mountain,
I am plummeting through space,
you may see this does not please me
by the frown upon my face.

As the ground keeps getting nearer,
it's a simple task to tell
that I've got a slight dilemma,
that my day's not going well.

My velocity's increasing,
I am dropping like a stone,
I could do with some assistance,
is there someone I can phone?

Though I'm unafraid of falling,
I am prompted to relate
that the landing has me worried,
and I don't have long to wait.

I am running out of options,
there's just one thing left to try –
in the next eleven seconds,
I have got to learn to fly!

Jack Prelutsky

THE PAINT BOX

'Cobalt and umber and ultramarine,
Ivory black and emerald green –
What shall I paint to give pleasure to you?'
'Paint for me somebody utterly new.'

'I have painted you tigers in crimson and white.'
'The colours were good and you painted aright.'
'I have painted the cook and camel in blue
And a panther in purple.' 'You painted them true.

Now mix me a colour that nobody knows,
And paint me a country where nobody goes,
And put in it people a little like you,
Watching a unicorn drinking the dew.'

E V Rieu

GRADE TWO *VERSE*

WATER MUSIC

There's an air of excitement deep under the waves;
there are sharks tuning up in the bottomless caves
for tonight there's a concert – they all take a part –
and each fish and each mollusc's rehearsing its art.
The upside-down-catfish conducts with his tail,
and the cymbals are clashed by a massive blue whale.
The clown fish, whose tenor is reedy and scratchy,
is practising solos from 'I Pagliacci'.
The haddock are plucking their strings pizzicato,
a rather large prawn's trying out 'The Mikado'.
There's a dolphin duet on piano and scuba.
A conger eel's trapped in the coils of a tuba.
Three plaice sing 'Titanic' in voices that quiver.
A rumble of bass harmonise 'Ole Man River'.
The halibut practise their scales with a screech
and the tuna's big drum can be heard up the beach.
Every sea slug, crab, jellyfish, cod will appear
to perform – it's the concert event of the year.

Alison Chisholm

MARMALADE

He's buried in the bushes,
with dockleaves round his grave,
A crimecat desperado
and his name was Marmalade.
He's the cat that caught the pigeon,
that stole the neighbour's meat...
and tore the velvet curtains
and stained the satin seat.
He's the cat that spoilt the laundry,

he's the cat that spilt the stew,
and chased the lady's poodle
and scratched her daughter too.

But –
No more we'll hear his cat flap,
or scratches at the door,
or see him at the window,
or hear his catnap snore.
So –
Ring his grave with pebbles,
erect a noble sign –
For here lies Marmalade
and Marmalade was MINE.

Peter Dixon

WATCH YOUR TEACHER CAREFULLY

It happened in school last week
when everything seemed fine
assembly, break, science and spelling
three twelves are four times nine.

But then I noticed my teacher
scratching the skin from her cheek
a forked tongue flicked from her lips
her nose hooked into a beak.

Her twenty arms grew longer
they ended in terrible claws
by now she was orange and yellow and green
with crunching great teeth in her jaws.

Her twenty eyes were upon me
as I ran from the room for the Head
got to his office, burst through the door
met a bloodsucking alien instead.

Somehow I got to the staffroom
the doorknob was dripping with slime
inside were seven hideous things
who thought I was dinner-time.

I made my escape through a window
just then a roaring sound
knocked me over flat on my face
as the whole school left the ground.

Powerful rockets pushed it
back into the darkest space
all I have left are the nightmares
and these feathers that grow on my face.

David Harmer

AT THE END OF A SCHOOL DAY

It is the end of a school day
  and down the long drive
come bag-swinging, shouting children.
  Deafened, the sky winces.
    The sun gapes in surprise.

Suddenly the runners skid to a stop,
  stand still and stare
at a small hedgehog
  curled up on the tarmac
    like an old, frayed cricket ball.

A girl dumps her bag, tiptoes forward
　and gingerly, so gingerly
carries the creature
　　to the safety of a shady hedge.
　　　Then steps back, watching.

Girl, children, sky and sun
　hold their breath.
There is silence,
　a moment to remember
　　on this warm afternoon in June.

Wes Magee

TIGER

He stalks in his vivid stripes
The few steps of his cage,
On pads of velvet quiet,
In his quiet rage.

He should be lurking in shadow,
Sliding through long grass,
Near the water hole
Where plump deer pass.

He should be snarling around houses
At the jungle's edge,
Baring his white fangs, his claws,
Terrorising the village!

But he's locked in a concrete cell,
His strength behind bars,
Stalking the length of his cage,
Ignoring visitors.

He hears the last voice at night,
The patrolling cars,
And stares with his brilliant eyes
At the brilliant stars.

Leslie Norris

THE SILVER FISH

While fishing in the blue lagoon,
I caught a lovely silver fish,
And he spoke to me, 'My boy,' quoth he,
'Please set me free and I'll grant your wish;
A kingdom of wisdom? A palace of gold?
Or all the fancies your mind can hold?'
And I said, 'O.K.,' and I set him free,
But he laughed at me as he swam away,
And left me whispering my wish
Into a silent sea.

Today I caught that fish again
(That lovely silver prince of fishes),
And once again he offered me,
If I would only set him free,
Any one of a number of wishes
If I would throw him back to the fishes.

He was delicious.

Shel Silverstein

THE SONG OF THE MISCHIEVOUS DOG

There are many who say that a dog has its day,
And a cat has a number of lives;
There are others who think that a lobster is pink,
And that bees never work in their hives.
There are fewer, of course, who insist that a horse
Has a horn and two humps on its head,
And a fellow who jests that a mare can build nests
Is as rare as a donkey that's red.
Yet in spite of all this, I have moments of bliss,
For I cherish a passion for bones,
And though doubtful of biscuit, I'm willing to risk it,
And I love to chase rabbits and stones.
But my greatest delight is to take a good bite
At a calf that is plump and delicious;
And if I indulge in a bite at a bulge,
Let's hope you won't think me too vicious.

Dylan Thomas

THE MAGIC BOX

I will put in the box

the swish of a silk sari on a summer night,
fire from the nostrils of a Chinese dragon,
the tip of a tongue touching a tooth.

I will put in the box

a snowman with a rumbling belly,
a sip of the bluest water from Lake Lucerne,
a leaping spark from an electric fish.

I will put in the box

three violet wishes spoken in Gujarati,
the last joke of an ancient uncle
and the first smile of a baby

I will put in the box

a fifth season and a black sun
a cowboy on a broomstick
and a witch on a white horse.

My box is fashioned from ice and gold and steel,
with stars on the lid and secrets in the corners.
Its hinges are the toe joints
of dinosaurs.

I shall surf on my box
on the great high-rolling breaks of the wild Atlantic,
then wash ashore on a yellow beach
the colour of the sun.

Kit Wright

GRADE TWO *PROSE*

THE LITTLE MERMAID
(a short story from *The Complete Fairy Tales and Stories*)

By morning the storm was over. Of the wrecked ship not a splinter was to be found. The sun rose, glowing red, and its rays gave colour to the young prince's cheeks but his eyes remained closed. The little mermaid kissed his forehead and stroked his wet hair. She thought that he looked like the statue in her garden. She kissed him again and wished passionately that he would live.

In the far distance she saw land; the mountains rose blue in the morning air. The snow on their peaks was as glittering white as swan's feathers. At the shore there was a green forest, and in its midst lay a cloister or a church, the little mermaid did not know which. Lemon and orange trees grew in the garden, and by the entrance gate stood a tall palm tree. There was a little bay nearby, where the water was calm and deep. The mermaid swam with her prince towards the beach. She laid him in the fine white sand, taking care to place his head in the warm sunshine far from the water.

In the big white buildings bells were ringing and a group of young girls was coming out to walk in the garden. The little mermaid swam out to some rocks and hid behind them. She covered her head with seaweed, so that she would not be noticed, while she waited to see who would find the poor prince.

Hans Christian Andersen

THE PEPPERMINT PIG

The milkman was saying, "...so the old sow farrowed early. D'you want a peppermint pig, Mrs Greengrass?"

Poll looked at him, thinking of sweets, but there was a real pig poking its snout out of the milkman's coat pocket. It was the tiniest pig she had ever seen. She touched its hard little head and said, "What's a peppermint pig?"

"Not worth much," Mother said. "Only a token. Like a peppercorn rent. Almost nothing."

"Runt of the litter," the milkman added. "Too small for the sow to raise. He'd only get trampled on in the rush."

Mother took the pig from him and held it firmly while it kicked and squealed piercingly. She tipped it to look at its stomach and said, "Well, he seems strong enough. And even runts grow."

The milkman took the jug from Poll and went to his cart to ladle milk out of his churn.

"Oh," Poll said. "Oh, *Mother*." She stroked the small, wriggling body. Stroked one way, its skin felt silky to touch; the other way, stiff little hairs prickled her fingers. He was a pale apricot colour all over.

The milkman came back. Mother said, "Will you take a shilling?" and he nodded and grinned. Poll took the milk to the kitchen and flew upstairs for her mother's purse. "Theo," she shouted, "look what we've got!"

Nina Bawden

THE ANGEL OF NITSHILL ROAD

Afterwards, no one could remember quite who it was who first guessed she was a real angel. There were enough clues, of course. Tracey overheard Mrs Brown complaining that Celeste had dropped 'out of the blue'. When Ian took the register to the school office he heard the secretary telling Miss Featherstone that the new girl had a 'heavenly' accent. And Mr Fairway was reported to have muttered that Celeste was having 'a bit of trouble coming down to earth'.

Then Lisa remembered that Celeste's father hadn't walked off that first morning. Or driven. He'd *flown*!

And that reminded Penny. How had Celeste's granny got there in time to stop her being given the wrong name?

She'd *swooped*.

The little group who chummed down Nitshill Road had a chat at the corner.

"So what did Celeste's father want to call her, anyway?"

Penny pushed the sweet she was sucking into the pouch of her cheek, out of the way.

"Angelica, she told us."

"*Angelica!*"

Another clue!

Anne Fine

THE VOYAGE OF THE DAWN TREADER

The things in the picture were moving. It didn't look at all like a cinema either; the colours were too real and clean and out-of-door for that. Down went the prow of the ship into the wave and up went a great shock of spray. And then up went the wave behind her, and her stern and her deck became visible for the first time, and then disappeared as the next wave came to meet her and her bows went up again. At the same moment an exercise book which had been lying beside Edmund on the bed flapped, rose and sailed through the air to the wall behind him, and Lucy felt all her hair whipping round her face as it does on a windy day. And this was a windy day; but the wind was blowing out of the picture towards them. And suddenly with the wind came the noises – the swishing of waves and the slap of water against the ship's sides and the creaking and the over-all high, steady roar of air and water. But it was the smell, the wild, briny smell, which really convinced Lucy that she was not dreaming.

"Stop it," came Eustace's voice, squeaky with fright and bad temper. "It's some silly trick you two are playing. Stop it. I'll tell Alberta – ow!"

The other two were much more accustomed to adventures, but, just exactly as Eustace Clarence said "Ow," they both said "Ow" too. The reason was that a great cold, salt splash had broken right out of the frame and they were breathless from the smack of it besides being wet through.

C S Lewis

THE GREAT PIRATICAL RUMBUSTIFICATION

All over the town the pirates were getting restless. "Yo, ho, ho!" they whispered in the lifts, the lofts and the lordly streets of the city.

These weren't the impulsive young pirates, mind you, but the older pirates who had retired from the sea to live on their ill-gotten riches.

That is why they were restless; it was months since there had been a pirate party.

The pirates were longing for Pirate Rum and for steaming bowls of Pirate Stew – a wonderful stew where every pirate puts something good into the pot...a turnip, a bunch of carrots, mushrooms or a bottle of wine.

It is a great piratical delicacy.

The sign of a pirate party is a message in the sky – the words 'Pirate Party', written over the stars.

Every night now the pirates studied the sky, but nothing was written there.

"O for a pirate party!" the pirates grumbled ominously, trying their swords for sharpness.

All the pirates – Roving Tom, Wild Jack Clegg, Rumbling Dick Rover, Orpheus Clinker and Old, Old, Oldest-of-all, Terrible Crabmeat – were restless with longing for a great Rumbust-ification.

The whole city was churning with restless pirates. The difficulty was that a pirate party must be a STOLEN one.

Margaret Mahy

A DOG SO SMALL

Ben turned eagerly from his family's presents to his post.

He turned over the letters first, looking for his grandfather's handwriting; but there was nothing. Then he looked at the writing on the two picture-postcards that had come for him – although you would hardly expect anything so important to be left to a postcard. There was nothing. Then he began to have the feeling that something might have gone wrong after all. He remembered, almost against his will, that his grandfather's promise had been only a whisper and a nod, and that not all promises are kept, anyway.

He turned to the parcels, and at once saw his grandfather's handwriting on a small flat one. Then he knew for certain that something was wrong. They would hardly send him an ordinary birthday present as well as one so special as a dog. There was only one explanation: they were sending him an ordinary present *instead of* the dog.

"Open it, Ben," said his mother; and his father reminded him, "Use your new knife on the string, boy." Ben never noticed the sharpness of the Sheffield steel as he cut the string round the parcel and then unfolded the wrapping-paper.

They had sent him a picture instead of a dog.

Philippa Pearce

A WALK IN WOLF WOOD

He dropped the medallion on top of the clothes. It went with a clink and a shimmer. "There. We can just leave the thing here for him to find, and go straight back. We've been far longer than we meant to. Daddy's probably fuming – or else he's on the way to meet us."

The thought was somehow rather cheering. It was, indeed, suddenly quite dark. The sun had set with great rapidity, and the crowding trees did the rest. The air was still warm, but the silence of the forest was deeper than before. The insect hum had faded. No bird called.

Except the owl. One hooted, whisperingly, far away among the pines. Then suddenly another answered, from quite near at hand. Not the whispering *tuwhoo* this time, but the dreadful screech that goes by in the night like murder, leaving the small creatures crouching, terrified, in their hiding places.

"Your watch must have stopped! Come *on!*" cried Margaret, and seizing John's hand pulled him towards the cottage door.

Then she screamed. John did not scream, but he made a sound like a shrill gasp with no breath in it. The two children, still holding hands, shrank backwards till they came right up against the bed.

In the cottage doorway, yellow eyes fixed and gleaming, jaws open and long tongue lolling, stood an enormous wolf.

Mary Stewart

JULIET'S STORY

Mr Addleripe had known Australian and American witches as well as Welsh witches. He'd known African witches who could kill you stone dead just by looking at you, and Egyptian and Norwegian witches and Sicilian witches. He'd known witches in Spain, Denmark, Hungary and France. Twenty-five years ago he'd known one in Greece. Actually, Mr Addleripe said, he'd made a study of witches.

A lot of nonsense was talked about witches, Mr Addleripe said. For a start, no witch ever flew about on a broomstick, nor did witches insist on living in the heart of a forest with only a black cat for company. And all films, stories and television programmes that claimed witches could be here one moment and gone the next were rubbish. There was no such thing as a disappearing witch. If you came across a woman who could disappear like that you were probably in the company of a ghost.

When first he'd talked to her about witches, Frances began to look for them.

"Oh no, no," he said when she told him that. "You'll never come across a witch easily, Frances. Your real witch doesn't go around showing off her powers, you know. Your real witch keeps quiet as a mouse about her powers. Naturally enough, Frances: time was, when you caught your witch you burned her."

William Trevor

GRADE THREE *VERSE*

SKATING

When I try to skate,
My feet are so wary
They grit and grate;
And then I watch Mary
Easily gliding,
Like an ice-fairy;
Skimming and curving,
Out and in,
With a turn of her head,
And a twirl and a spin;
Sailing under
The breathless hush
Of the willows, and back
To the frozen rush;
Out to the island
And round the edge,
Skirting the rim
Of the crackling sedge,
Swerving close
To the poplar root,
And round the lake
On a single foot,
With a three, and an eight,
And a loop and a ring;
Where Mary glides,
The lake will sing!
Out in the mist
I hear her now
Under the frost
Of the willow-bough

Easily sailing,
Light and fleet
With the song of the lake
beneath her feet.

Herbert Asquith

MY MOTHER SAW A DANCING BEAR

My mother saw a dancing bear
By the schoolyard, a day in June.
The keeper stood with chain and bar
And whistle-pipe, and played a tune.

And bruin lifted up its head
And lifted up its dusty feet,
And all the children laughed to see
It caper in the summer heat.

They watched as for the Queen it died.
They watched it march. They watched it halt.
They heard the keeper as he cried,
'Now, roly-poly!' 'Somersault!'

And then, my mother said, there came
The keeper with a begging-cup,
The bear with burning coat of fur,
Shaming the laughter to a stop.

They paid a penny for the dance,
But what they saw was not the show;
Only, in bruin's aching eyes,
Far-distant forests, and the snow.

Charles Causley

DAYDREAMS

My mum loved
The colour blue
And barley-sugars, rum and coke,

Mustard on her kippers, bowls of tripe,
Coronation Street and TV games.
Whist and rummy, bingo, beetle drives,

A movie star with eyes like hard-boiled eggs.
Waltzing round the kitchen, singing hymns,
And shouting at my dad.

And she loved to daydream.
I can see her now, sitting by the fire,
Gazing at the flames and shadows there.

Though what she saw in them I never knew
I thought her secret died along with her.
Till now. Till my dreams came.

And now I know just what it was she dreamed.
It was her own mum she could see
Years ago, dreaming just like her, like me.

Berlie Doherty

WOLF

Yesterday, in Crawley, I saw a white alsatian
And out of my childhood memories leaped Wolf
The huge white alsatian that terrified me
Every time I walked down Priors Road
Sent by my mum on some errand to the shop.
They say animals can smell your fear;

Wolf seemed to know I was coming
Before I even left our house.
He would lie straddled across the pavement
Like some great battleship,
Or lurk shark-like, in the dark
Passageway between the houses where he lived
Ready to rise up and challenge me
With deep-throated barks that threatened invasion.
I had witnessed his ferocity when he had
Ambushed and demolished other dogs
So I would cross the road to avoid him
Hoping that someone else, or a car,
Would come between us.
Or, when I got to the corner and spied him,
I would turn back to tell my mum
That the shop was closed.

Chris Eddershaw

PIGEONS

They paddle with staccato feet
In powder-pools of sunlight,
Small blue busybodies
Strutting like fat gentlemen
With hands clasped
Under their swallowtail coats;
And, as they stump about,
Their heads like tiny hammers
Tap at imaginary nails
In non-existent walls.
Elusive ghosts of sunshine
Slither down the green gloss
Of their necks an instant, and are gone.

Summer hangs drugged from sky to earth
In limpid fathoms of silence:
Only warm dark dimples of sound
Slide like slow bubbles
From the contented throats.

Raise a casual hand –
With one quick gust
They fountain into air.

Richard Kell

BAD DAY AT THE ARK

On the eleventh morning
Japheth burst into the cabin:
'Dreadful news, everybody, the tigers
have eaten the bambanolas!'

'Oh, not the bambanolas,' cried Mrs Noah.
'But they were my favourites,
all cuddly and furry,
and such beautiful brown eyes.'

Noah took her hand in his.
'Momma, not only were they cute
but they could sing and dance
and speak seven languages.'

'And when baked, their dung was delicious,'
added Shem wistfully.
Everybody agreed that the earth
would be a poorer place without the bambanolas.

Noah determined to look on the bright side.
'At least we still have the quinquasaurapods.'
'Oh, yes, the darling creatures,' said his wife.
'How would we manage without them?'

On deck, one quinquasaurapod was steering,
cooking, fishing, doing a crossword
and finding a cure for cancer.
The other was being stalked by a tiger.

Roger McGough

WIND-UP

Gagged on silence, with a look
Of terror in its little eyes,
The clockwork bird has lost its song
And cannot find out what went wrong
However hard it tries.

Broken-hearted, half-way through
The triumph of a gorgeous trill –
The universe seemed filled with sound
Then something juddered, thumped, unwound
And suddenly stopped still.

What a shame. It worked last year.
A Christmas bird should always sing.
Indeed it should, but so life goes
With all our bright arpeggios
Dependent on a spring,

And there it looks down from its branch
With empty throat and beak ajar
While underneath the glittering tree
A child who might have once been me
Winds up his brand new car.

John Mole

A HOT DAY

Cottonwool clouds loiter.
A lawnmower, very far,
Birrs. Then a bee comes
To a crimson rose and softly,
Deftly and fatly crams
A velvet body in.

A tree, June-lazy, makes
A tent of dim green light.
Sunlight weaves in the leaves,
Honey-light laced with leaf-light,
Green interleaved with gold.
Sunlight gathers its rays
In sheaves, which the wind unweaves
And then reweaves – the wind
That puffs a smell of grass
Through the heat-heavy, trembling
Summer pool of air.

A S J Tessimond

GRADE THREE *PROSE*

THE CUCKOO SISTER

We came out of the dark alley into a blaze of colour. We were in a market. Stalls lined the street on either side. Fruit and vegetables, old clothes and new china. Handbags and leather belts. Pink nylon, flowered cotton, silver bracelets from India, glass beads from Birmingham.

"Mind out!" a man said, as I slipped on a squashed cabbage leaf and bumped against his stall. Then he caught sight of Rosie. "Hullo, sweetheart. Haven't seen you around lately. Bin on your holidays?"

"No. You ain't seen my mum, have you?" she asked.

"Your mum? Can't say I 'ave. Not today."

"What about yesterday? Or the day before?"

His small eyes were suddenly sharp. "'Ow long she bin gone, Rosie love?" he asked, not unkindly. "She ain't left you on yer own, 'as she?"

"No. It's all right," Rosie said, wriggling her shoulders. "I just wondered if you'd seen her about, that's all."

He looked at her, rubbing his thumb over his chin thoughtfully. Then he shouted, "Hey, Elsie, 'ave you seen Louise Martin around lately?"

The woman at the next stall (Towels and sheets), turned around. I don't think she noticed us. Her round face assumed an expression of enjoyable gloom.

"'Aven't you 'eard?" she asked, seeming unable to believe her luck. "She's gone off. Left 'er little girl locked in 'er room. Tied to a bedpost. Starving she was when they found 'er, poor little mite."

The man, embarrassed, tried to stop her but it was no good. She was in full spate.

Vivien Alcock

SKELLIG

Dust poured through the torch beam. Something scratched and scratched in a corner. I tiptoed further in and felt spider webs breaking my brow. Everything was packed in tight – ancient furniture, kitchen units, rolled-up carpets, pipes and crates and planks. I kept ducking down under the hosepipes and ropes and kitbags that hung from the roof. More cobwebs snapped on my clothes and skin. The floor was broken and crumbly. I opened a cupboard an inch, shone the torch in and saw a million woodlice scattering away. I peered down into a great stone jar and saw the bones of some little animal that had died in there. Dead bluebottles were everywhere. There were ancient newspapers and magazines. I shone the torch on to one and saw that it came from nearly fifty years ago. I moved so carefully. I was scared every moment that the whole thing was going to collapse. There was dust clogging my throat and nose. I knew they'd be yelling for me soon and I knew I'd better get out. I leaned across a heap of tea chests and shone the torch into the space behind and that's when I saw him.

I thought he was dead. He was sitting with his legs stretched out, and his head tipped back against the wall. He was covered in dust and webs like everything else and his face was thin and pale. Dead bluebottles were scattered on his hair and shoulders. I shone the torch on his white face and his black suit.

"What do you want?" he said.

He opened his eyes and looked up at me.

His voice squeaked like he hadn't used it in years.

"What do you want?"

David Almond

KING OF SHADOWS

"Look out!" I said, and I stood behind Roper, put my arms round him, made a fist with one hand between his ribs and his belly-button, put my other hand over it and jerked in and upward, hard. So the air was pushed up out of Roper's lungs, up through his windpipe, and the piece of apple popped out. It fell out of his mouth and he hung there over my arm, making awful noises, great croaking gasps for air. But he was breathing.

The voices from the stage went echoing on around us, but everyone backstage was staring at me. I looked at them, and felt uneasy; they looked almost as scared as they had when he was choking.

Nick said, amazed, "What did you do?"

I guess I babbled, because I was nervous. I said, "It's called the Heimlich manoeuvre, some guy called Heimlich invented it – " And they went on staring, and I realised too late that I was sounding completely like a modern kid, because in Elizabethan England they didn't use the word guy or probably the word manoeuvre either, and how could they know who Mr Heimlich was, when he wasn't going to be born for hundreds of years yet?

I said lamely, "My aunt showed me how."

Then Roper rescued me. He threw up on the floor.

Susan Cooper

WILLIAM AGAIN

The robing of William himself as the villain had cost him much care and thought. He had finally decided upon the drawing-room rug pinned across his shoulder and a fern-pot upon his head. It was a black china fern-pot and rather large, but it rested upon William's ears, and gave him a commanding and sinister appearance. He also carried an umbrella.

These preparations took longer than the cast had foreseen, and, when finally large moustaches had been corked upon the hero's, villain's and crowd's lips, the lunch-bell sounded from the hall.

"Jus' all finished in time!" said William the optimist.

"Yes, but wot about the rehearsal," said the crowd gloomily, "wot about that?"

"Well, you've had the book to learn the stuff," said William, "that's enough, isn't it? I don't s'pose real acting people bother with rehearsals. It's quite easy. You jus' learn your stuff an' then say it. It's silly wasting time over rehearsals."

"Have you learnt wot you say, William Brown?" said the heroine shrilly.

"I *know* wot I say," said William loftily, "I don't need to *learn*!"

"William!" called a stern sisterly voice from the house, "mother says come and get ready for lunch."

William merely ejected his tongue in the direction of the voice and made no answer.

Richmal Crompton

STORMBREAKER

Alex glanced at his watch. About three minutes had passed since Crawley had left the office, and he had said he would be back in five. If he was going to find anything here, he had to find it quickly. He pulled open a drawer of the desk. It contained five or six thick files. Alex took them and opened them. He saw at once that they had nothing to do with banking.

The first was marked: NERVE POISONS – NEW METHODS OF CONCEALMENT AND DISSEMINATION. Alex put it aside and looked at the second. ASSASSINATIONS – FOUR CASE STUDIES. Growing ever more puzzled, he quickly flicked through the rest of the files, which covered counter-terrorism, the movement of uranium across Europe and interrogation techniques. The last file was simply labelled: STORMBREAKER.

Alex was about to read it when the door suddenly opened and two men walked in. One of them was Crawley. The other was the driver from the breaker's yard. Alex knew there was no point trying to explain what he was doing. He was sitting behind the desk with the Stormbreaker file open in his hands. But at the same time he realized that the two men weren't surprised to see him there. From the way they had come into the room, they had expected to find him.

"This isn't a bank," Alex said. "Who are you? Was my uncle working for you? Did you kill him?"

"So many questions," Crawley muttered. "But I'm afraid we're not authorized to give you the answers."

The other man lifted his hand and Alex saw that he was holding a gun.

Anthony Horowitz

THE PHANTOM TOLLBOOTH

"SILENCE!" thundered the policeman, pulling himself up to full height and glaring menacingly at the terrified bug. "And now," he continued, speaking to Milo, "where were you on the night of 27 July?"

"What does that have to do with it?" asked Milo.

"It's my birthday, that's what," said the policeman as he entered "Forgot my birthday" in his little book. "Boys always forget other people's birthdays.

"You have committed the following crimes," he continued. "Having a dog with an unauthorized alarm, sowing confusion, upsetting the applecart, wreaking havoc, and mincing words."

"Now see here," growled Tock angrily.

"And illegal barking," he added, frowning at the watchdog. "It's against the law to bark without using the barking meter. Are you ready to be sentenced?"

"Only a judge can sentence you," said Milo, who remembered reading that in one of his schoolbooks.

"Good point," replied the policeman, taking off his cap and putting on a long black robe. "I am also the judge. Now would you like a long or a short sentence?"

"A short one, if you please," said Milo.

"Good," said the judge, rapping his gavel three times. "I always have trouble remembering the long ones. How about 'I am'? That's the shortest sentence I know."

Everyone agreed that it was a very fair sentence, and the judge continued: "There will also be a small additional penalty of six million years in prison. Case closed," he pronounced.

Norton Juster

THE AMBER SPYGLASS

She looked back again at the foul and dismal shore, so bleak and blasted with disease and poison, and thought of her dear Pan waiting there alone, her heart's companion, watching her disappear into the mist, and she fell into a storm of weeping. Her passionate sobs didn't echo, because the mist muffled them, but all along the shore in innumerable ponds and shallows, in wretched broken tree stumps, the damaged creatures that lurked there heard her full-hearted cry and drew themselves a little closer to the ground, afraid of such passion.

"If he could come –" cried Will, desperate to end her grief, but the boatman shook his head.

"He can come in the boat, but if he does, the boat stays here," he said.

"But how will she find him again?"

"I don't know."

"When we leave, will we come back this way?"

"Leave?"

"We're going to come back. We're going to the land of the dead and we are going to come back."

"Not this way."

"Then some other way, but we will!"

"I have taken millions, and none came back."

"Then we shall be the first. We'll find our way out. And since we're going to do that, be kind, boatman, be compassionate, let her take her dæmon!"

"No," he said and shook his ancient head. "It's not a rule you can break."

Philip Pullman

HOLES

A sign on the door said WRECK ROOM.

Nearly everything in the room was broken; the TV, the pinball machine, the furniture. Even the people looked broken, with their worn-out bodies sprawled over the various chairs and sofas.

X-Ray and Armpit were playing pool. The surface of the table reminded Stanley of the surface of the lake. It was full of bumps and holes because so many people had carved their initials into the felt.

There was a hole in the far wall, and an electric fan had been placed in front of it. Cheap air-conditioning. At least the fan worked.

As Stanley made his way across the room, he tripped over an outstretched leg.

"Hey, watch it!" said an orange lump on a chair.

"You watch it," muttered Stanley, too tired to care.

"What'd you say?" the Lump demanded.

"Nothin'," said Stanley.

The Lump rose. He was almost as big as Stanley and a lot tougher. "You said something." He poked his fat finger in Stanley's neck. "What'd you say?"

A crowd quickly formed around them.

"Be cool," said X-Ray. He put his hand on Stanley's shoulder. "You don't want to mess with the Caveman," he warned.

"The Caveman's cool," said Armpit.

"I'm not looking for trouble," Stanley said. "I'm just tired, that's all."

The Lump grunted.

X-Ray and Armpit led Stanley over to a couch. Squid slid over to make room as Stanley sat down.

"Did you see the Caveman back there?" X-Ray asked.

"The Caveman's one tough dude," said Squid, and he lightly punched Stanley's arm.

Louis Sachar

GRADE FOUR *VERSE*

ABOUT HIS PERSON

Five pounds fifty in change, exactly,
a library card on its date of expiry.

A postcard, stamped,
unwritten, but franked,

a pocket-size diary slashed with a pencil
from March twenty-fourth to the first of April.

A brace of keys for a mortise lock,
an analogue watch, self-winding, stopped.

A final demand
in his own hand,

a rolled-up note of explanation
planted there like a spray carnation

but beheaded, in his fist.
A shopping list.

A giveaway photograph stashed in his wallet,
a keepsake banked in the heart of a locket.

No gold or silver,
but crowning one finger

a ring of white unweathered skin.
That was everything.

Simon Armitage

CALLING IN THE CAT

Now from the dark, a deeper dark,
The cat slides,
Furtive and aware,
His eyes still shine with meteor spark
The cold dew weights his hair.
Suspicious,
Hesitant, he comes
Stepping morosely from the night,
Held but repelled,
Repelled but held,
By lamp and firelight.

Now call your blandest,
Offer up
The sacrifice of meat,
And snare the wandering soul with greeds,
Give him to drink and eat,
And he shall walk fastidiously
Into the trap of old
On feet that still smell delicately
Of withered ferns and mould.

Elizabeth Coatsworth

TICH MILLER

Tich Miller wore glasses
with Elastoplast-pink frames
and had one foot three sizes larger than the other.

When they picked teams for outdoor games
she and I were always the last two
left standing by the wire-mesh fence.

We avoided one another's eyes,
stooping, perhaps, to re-tie a shoelace,
or affecting interest in the flight

of some fortunate bird, and pretended
not to hear the urgent conference:
'Have Tubby!' 'No, no, have Tich!'

Usually they chose me, the lesser dud,
and she lolloped, unselected,
to the back of the other team.

At eleven we went to different schools.
In time I learned to get my own back,
Sneering at hockey-players who couldn't spell.

Tich died when she was twelve.

Wendy Cope

PAINT

A dumpy plain-faced child stands gazing there,
One hand laid lightly on a purple chair.
Her stuffed and stone-grey gown is laced with black;
A chain, with pendant star, hangs round her neck.
Red bows deck wrist and breast and flaxen hair;
Shoulder to waist's a band of lettered gold.
Round eyes, and cupid mouth – say, seven years old;
The ghost of her father in her placid stare.
Darkness beyond; bold lettering overhead:
L'INFANTA, MARGUERITE, there I read;
And wondered – tongue-tied mite, and shy, no doubt –
What grave Velásquez talked to her about.

Walter de la Mare

APPLEMOON

Something woke me: startle-sound
or moonlight. The house dreamt
like an old cat, but I
looked out my window.

And night was day in a midnight
moon-flood. Mazy moon
flaring a halo of quick clouds
running the big black sky.
And I saw a thousand windfall apples
lying luminous as sea-stones beached
below the spiky silver trees.

So, shivering I
mouse-went out
with a basket, barefoot, toes
curling in the cold;
and singing soft
took ripe reluctant apples
under close and curious stars.

Only soon I saw
my shadow was not
the same as I;
it stooped more –
had its own thinness…
and our fingers
never met.

I quick-ran back
the house so
sleepy-warm, sure.
But looking out through the curtain lace

I saw my shadow linger
moving slow and crooked, plucking
shadow apples
from the shining moony grass.

Rose Flint

THE NEW FOAL

Yesterday he was nowhere to be found
In the skies or under the skies.

Suddenly he's here – a warm heap
Of ashes and embers, fondled by small draughts.

A star dived from outer space – flared
And burned out in the straw.
Now something is stirring in the smoulder.
We call it a foal.

Still stunned
He has no idea where he is.
His eyes, dew-dusky, explore gloom walls and a glare
doorspace.
Is this the world?
It puzzles him. It is a great numbness.

He pulls himself together, getting used to the weight of things
And to that tall horse nudging him, and to this straw.

Ted Hughes

JABBERMOCKERY

'Twas Thursday and the naughty girls
Did gyre and gimble in the gym.
All mimsy was Miss Borogrove
And Mr Maths was grim.

'Beware the Number Man, my friend!
His sums that snarl. His co-ordinates that catch!
Beware the Deputy Bird, and shun
The evil Earring snatch!'

She took her ballpoint pen in hand:
Long time the problem's end she sought –
So rested she by the lavatory
And sat awhile in thought.

And as in toughish thought she sat,
The Number Man with eyes of flame
Came calculating through the cloakroom doors
And subtracted as he came.

She thought real fast as he went past;
The well-placed soap went slickersmack!
She left him stunned and with the sums
She went galumphing back.

'And has thou got the answers, Jackie?
Come to our desk,' beamed idle boys.
'Oh, frabjous day, Quelle heure! Calais!'
They chortled in their joy.

'Twas Thursday and the naughty girls
Did gyre and gimble in the gym.
All mimsy was Miss Borogrove
And Mr Maths was grim.

Trevor Millum

BORING

I'm dead bored,
> bored to the bone.
Nobody likes me,
> I'm all alone.
I'll just go crawl
> under a stone.

Hate my family,
> got no friends,
I'll sit here till
> the universe ends
Or I starve to death –
> it all depends.

Then I'll be dead,
> dead and rotten,
Less than a blot when
> it's been well blotten,
Less than a teddy bear
> that's been forgotten.

Then I'll go to Heaven which
> is more than can be said
For certain persons
> when they're dead.
They'll go you-know-
> where instead.

Then they'll be sorry,
> Then they'll be glum,
Sitting on a stove till
> Kingdom Come.
Then they can all go
> kiss my...

Hmm, that's a sort of swearing;
    people shouldn't swear.
I won't go to Heaven but
    I don't care,
    I don't care,
    I don't care.
I'll sit here and swear
    so there.

Except that it's boring...

John Whitworth

GRADE FOUR *PROSE*

ARTHUR: AT THE CROSSING-PLACES

The knights of the Round Table hold their noses; the ladies bury their faces in their sleeves as they pass the wounded man, the Knight Without a Name, lying in the chamber that leads to the hall.

A snapped sword-blade is sticking through the knight's rotting rib-cage. Barbed arrow-tips are embedded in his neck, his stomach.

"If no one here can heal my wounds," the knight says quietly, "I will soon die."

But no one can. Neither Sir Gawain nor Sir Balin, not Sir Tor or his father King Pellinore. Not the ladies who feel the knight's pain as if it were their own. Not even the healers or teachers at King Arthur's court.

"The only man who can heal me," says the Knight Without a Name, "is the one who swears to avenge me. He must fight every single man loyal to the knight who gave me these wounds."

"No one here can do that," Arthur-in-the-stone tells his knights. "Who knows what that might lead to?"

Now there's a rumpus at the hall door: Nimue has returned to court. The moment Merlin sees her, he sighs and hurries down to meet her. He is almost old; she is almost young. He cannot help himself.

Behind Nimue, there's a young man, and I like the look of him. His brow is broad and his eyes are like Tom's eyes, blue and amused. His horse is white, he's wearing a white woollen cloak, and the sword slung around his neck has a white scabbard. His shield, though, is blue as lapis lazuli, and has three gold lions prancing across it.

Kevin Crossley-Holland

CORAM BOY

"Tommy!" a voice hissed from behind the pillar. A small bare-footed girl peered round shyly carrying a bundle in her apron. "Our mam's sent some clothes for you. Wants for you to look like a gentleman." She giggled at the thought.

Thomas peeled away from the choir, embarrassed. He pulled his little sister out of sight. "What are you doing here, Lizzy?" he asked roughly.

"Mam wanted you to be dressed proper for going away. She sent you these." Lizzie thrust a bundle into his arms, wrapped in a piece of sail cloth.

Thomas wondered how his mother could possibly afford to send anything decent that he could wear. He had intended going in the clothes provided by the cathedral: his choir school breeches, stockings and tailed jacket.

He prised open a corner and peeped inside. There was a jacket and breeches made of sturdy broadcloth, a shirt of not too coarse a cotton and a woven waistcoat. He looked up, puzzled. "How did she come by these?"

Lizzie giggled again. "They were our uncle Martin's clothes. You don't mind, do you? Mam thought you would fit them now – being as how you're the same age he was when he died."

"Thanks, Liz," he dropped a kiss on her bonneted head. "Thank Ma for me, and tell her I'll take care of the clothes. Now, go – or you'll get into trouble."

"Tommy – are you going to be a gentleman?" teased Lizzie. "You will come home and tell us all about it, won't you? You'll never be too grand for us, will you?"

"Shoo – you silly little goose," laughed Thomas, and pushed her off. "And don't forget to give our mam a big kiss from me," he called after her.

Jamila Gavin

THE NATURE OF THE BEAST

I knew.

I was the only person in Haverston that knew, and I wasn't telling. How can I make you understand why I didn't tell anyone? First on, there was the flame, the temper, in my guts. Second, more important, that one bit of knowing was like the only power I'd ever had. No one had given it to me and no one could take it away. It was dangerous and it was mine. It was a secret, and as long as it stayed my secret, it was my power, because whoever has the secrets has the power, I reckon.

And thirdly, nobody would have believed me. People only seem to believe me when I'm lying – when I tell the truth they mostly laugh or ignore me.

I expect if anyone was watching me they'd have thought I'd gone stark staring bonkers! I was gawping, terrified, at this little black cat sitting on a wall, washing its whiskers. My feet wouldn't move. Nothing would move, and all the hair on the back of my head began to creep. I'm not lying. It really does stand on end, well, creep, when you're scared witless.

Or maybe I was witless already. Some folks will think I was.

I turned around, went back into town and straight to the library.

"I want a book on cats," I said.

Silly old blighter gave me a book about moggies, but it was all right because on the same shelf I found what I was looking for.

I flicked through the pages of this big book, then I closed it with a bang. Some people looked at me.

It was black.

It was a panther.

I didn't read any more. I shut the book, because the Beast was staring at me out of the page.

I recognized him, but I didn't want him to recognize me.

I don't remember walking home.

Janni Howker

JOURNEY TO THE RIVER SEA

In the evening, when Miss Minton came to 'hear her read', Maia said, "I'm not staying here without you. I shall write to Mr Murray."

"I think you will find that at the salary the Carters are paying me, it might take a little while to find someone else," said Miss Minton dryly. She picked up Maia's hairbrush. "Don't tell me you're doing a hundred strokes a night because I don't believe it. I've told you again and again that you must look after your hair." She picked up the brush and brushed fiercely for a while. And then: "Do you want to go back, Maia? Back to England?"

"I did," she said, thinking about it. "The twins are so awful and there seemed no point in being here, shut up in this house. But not now. I don't want to go now because I've seen that it is there. What I thought was there."

Miss Minton waited.

"I mean…the forest…the river…the Amazon…everything I thought of before I came. And the people who live in it and know about it."

Then she told Miss Minton about the boy who had taken her into Manaus.

"He didn't speak English, but he had such a listening face; I couldn't believe he didn't understand everything I said. Oh, Minty, it was such a wonderful journey, like floating through a drowned forest. You can't believe it's the same world as the Carters live in."

"It isn't," said Miss Minton. "People make their own worlds."

Eva Ibbotson

TUG OF WAR

In spite of the proximity of battle, Tomas and Zigi continued to roam the fields, chewing strands of grass when their stomachs ached with hunger. They took their fishing tackle and fished along the riverbank. Some days they returned triumphant, carrying a little fish or two which their mothers grilled on the stove and divided up so that everyone could have a taste, although often that taste seemed to make them more conscious of their hunger. Their clothes hung slackly on them now.

One afternoon, when the boys were fishing, they worked their way further up river than usual to where a road bridge spanned it. Zigi had just pulled out a small perch and was yelling with excitement when Tomas saw movement up ahead.

"Shush, Zig! Soldiers!"

The soldiers in their grey-green German uniforms were working with something near the bridge. Several had gone underneath.

"Explosives!" said Tomas. "They're going to blow up the bridge."

"What for?" asked Zigi, his eyes opening wide.

They crawled a little nearer on their stomachs, to watch through the long grass.

"To stop the Americans getting through," whispered Tomas. "They can't be far away, Father says."

At that moment, they heard the whine of aircraft overhead and saw, coming in low, half a dozen U.S. fighter planes.

"Run," cried Tomas.

They hardly had time to drop their lines and their hooked fish and take to their heels before the world erupted round them. This is what hell must be like, thought Tomas, as he ran, panting, faster than he'd ever run in his life. They were running *for* their lives.

Joan Lingard

THE WIND SINGER

The scarlet-robed official arrived at the base of the wind singer.

"You, boy," he said sharply to Bowman. "What's she doing? Who is she?"

"She's my sister," said Bowman.

"And who are you?"

"I'm her brother."

The fierce official made him nervous, and when nervous, Bowman became very logical. Momentarily baffled, the official looked up and called to Kestrel:

"Get down, girl! Get down at once! What do you think you're doing up there?"

"Pongo!" Kestrel called back, climbing ever higher up the structure.

"What?" said the official. "What did she say?"

"Pongo," said Bowman.

"She said pongo to me?"

"I'm not sure," said Bowman. "She might have been saying it to me."

"But it was I who spoke to her. I ordered her to come down, and she replied, pongo."

"Perhaps she thinks it's your name."

"It's not my name. No one is called Pongo."

"I didn't know that. I expect she doesn't know that."

The official, confused by Bowman's tremulous but reasonable manner, turned his face back up to Kestrel, who was now almost at the very top, and called out:

"Did you say pongo to me?"

"Pongo pooa-pooa pompaprune!" Kestrel called back.

The official turned to Bowman, his face rigid with righteousness.

"There! You heard her! It's a disgrace!" He called back up to Kestrel, "If you don't come down, I'll report you!"

"You'll report her even if she does come down," said Bowman.

"I certainly shall," said the official, "but I shall report her more if she doesn't." He shouted up at Kestrel, "I shall recommend that points be deducted from your family rating!"

"Bangaplop!" called Kestrel.

William Nicholson

THE RINALDI RING

The room seemed smaller, somehow. The walls loomed in at him, patterned with tiny flowers, drenched in perfume. And all at once it came to him. Mary-Ellen slept here, in this room. Or lay awake, recalling some precious time when a soldier stood outside the house, calling her name. Would she have looked through the bars? Why were they there? "They had to lock her up," the dentist had said. Was this room her prison, then?

Eliot swung his feet out of bed and went to the window. The street outside was deserted. It must have been well after midnight. A few cars rolled down the High Street. The night was muggy and starless. A sound began in the distance and swelled until it seemed to be entering Fly Street: a crunching, rhythmic drumming. It billowed closer, not thunder or machinery of any sort; it had an unresisting dreadful doggedness, and as it crescendoed towards Eliot he recognized the beat of marching feet. As they passed the house, he saw them: a regiment of ghostly volunteers in dull khaki. He saw their glinting regimental badges, their backs braided with canvas straps, leather holsters and bayonets. One man looked up at Eliot and gave a bleak smile. His eyes were hidden by his peaked hat.

And then they were gone.

Jenny Nimmo

FACE

He controlled his eyelids, opening them just enough to let his eyes get used to the idea of light. His eyelids flickered. For a moment he stared at his own eyelashes and as he continued his slow opening, he heard a scream.

"Aaarrrgh, Clive, he's waking up, I saw his eyes. Move, Clive, he's waking up."

"OK, Wendy. It's all right," Martin's father said in a whisper.

Martin opened his eyes fully. At first he looked straight ahead. He could see clearly but he could not see much, only the hospital ceiling. He closed his eyes once more; now he started a body check. He moved his toes, and tensed his calf muscles and his thigh muscles. He moved his whole left leg no more than a quarter of an inch and then his right leg. It was the smallest of movements but all he wanted to know was that he was in control. By now there was more movement in his fingers, and again, a very small movement of his arms satisfied him. He breathed in deeply and his chest rose. Now Martin opened his eyes again, trying as he did so to raise his eyebrows but there was absolutely no feeling there. He tried to smile but he could feel only a hard skin which he seemed unable to control. He tried to move his jaw from side to side but the skin seemed inflexible and his jaw wouldn't move.

At this point Martin knew that something terrible had happened to his face.

Benjamin Zephaniah

GRADE FIVE *VERSE*

MRS REECE LAUGHS

Laughter, with us, is no great undertaking,
A sudden wave that breaks and dies in breaking.
Laughter, with Mrs Reece is much less simple:
It germinates, it spreads, dimple by dimple,
From small beginnings, things of easy girth,
To formidable redundancies of mirth.
Clusters of subterranean chuckles rise
And presently the circles of her eyes
Close into slits and all the woman heaves
As a great elm with all its mounds of leaves
Wallows before the storm. From hidden sources
A mustering of blind volcanic forces
Takes her and shakes her till she sobs and gapes.
Then all that load of bottled mirth escapes
In one wild crow, a lifting of huge hands,
And creaking stays, a visage that expands
In scarlet ridge and furrow. Thence collapse,
A hanging head, a feeble hand that flaps
An apron-end to stir an air and waft
A streaming face. And Mrs Reece has laughed.

Martin Armstrong

THE TYGER

Tyger! Tyger! burning bright
In the forests of the night,
What immortal hand or eye
Could frame thy fearful symmetry?

In what distant deeps or skies
Burnt the fire of thine eyes?
On what wings dare he aspire?
What the hand dare sieze the fire?

And what shoulder, & what art,
Could twist the sinews of thy heart?
And when thy heart began to beat,
What dread hand? & what dread feet?

What hammer? what the chain?
In what furnace was thy brain?
What the anvil? what dread grasp
Dare its deadly terrors clasp?

When the stars threw down their spears,
And water'd heaven with their tears,
Did he smile his work to see?
Did he who made the Lamb make thee?

Tyger! Tyger! burning bright
In the forests of the night,
What immortal hand or eye
Dare frame thy fearful symmetry?

William Blake

AT THE THEATRE
To the Lady Behind Me

Dear Madam, you have seen this play;
I never saw it till today.
You know the details of the plot,
But, let me tell you, I do not.
The author seeks to keep from me
The murderer's identity,
And you are not a friend of his
If you keep shouting who it is.
The actors in their funny way
Have several funny things to say,

But they do not amuse me more
If you have said them just before;
The merit of the drama lies,
I understand, in some surprise;
But the surprise must now be small
Since you have just foretold it all.
The lady you have brought with you
Is, I infer, a half-wit too,
But I can understand the piece
Without assistance from your niece.
In short, foul woman, it would suit
Me just as well if you were mute;
In fact, to make my meaning plain,
I trust you will not speak again.
And – may I add one human touch?–
Don't breathe upon my neck so much.

A P Herbert

WAITING FOR THE BIRDIE

Some hate broccoli, some hate bacon,
I hate having my picture taken.
How can your family claim to love you
And then demand a picture of you?
The electric chair is a queasy chair,
But I know an equally comfortless pair;
One is the dentist's, my good sirs,
And the other is the photographer's.
Oh, the fly in all domestic ointments
Is affectionate people who make appointments
To have your teeth filled left and right,
Or your face reproduced in black and white.

You open the door and you enter the studio,
And you feel less cheerio than nudio.
The hard light shines like seventy suns,
And you know that your features are foolish ones.
The photographer says, Natural, please,
And you cross your knees and uncross your knees.
Like a duke in a high society chronicle
The camera glares at you through its monocle
And you feel ashamed of your best attire,
Your nose itches, your palms perspire,
Your muscles stiffen, and all the while
You smile and smile and smile and smile.
It's over; you weakly grope for the door;
It's not; the photographer wants one more.
And if this experience you survive,
Wait, just wait till the proofs arrive.
You look like a drawing by Thurber or Bab,
Or a gangster stretched on a marble slab.
And all your dear ones, including your wife,
Say There he is, that's him to the life!
Some hate broccoli, some hate bacon,
But I hate having my picture taken.

Ogden Nash

THE RIVER'S STORY

I remember when life was good.
I shilly-shallied across meadows,
Tumbled down mountains,
I laughed and gurgled through woods,
Stretched and yawned in a myriad of floods.
Insects, weightless as sunbeams,
Settled upon my skin to drink.

I wore lily-pads like medals.
Fish, lazy and battled-scarred,
Gossiped beneath them.
The damselflies were my ballerinas,
The pike my ambassadors.
Kingfishers, disguised as rainbows,
Were my secret agents.
It was a sweet time, a gone-time,
A time before factories grew,
Brick by greedy brick,
And left me cowering
In monstrous shadows.
Like drunken giants
They vomited their poisons into me.
Tonight a scattering of vagrant bluebells,
Dwarfed by the same poisons,
Toll my ending.
Children, come and find me if you wish,
I am your inheritance.
Behind the derelict housing-estates
You will discover my remnants.
Clogged with garbage and junk
To an open sewer I've shrunk.
I, who have flowed through history,
Who have seen hamlets become villages,
Villages become towns, towns become cities,
Am reduced to a trickle of filth
Beneath the still, burning stars.

Brian Patten

GRANNIE

I stayed with her when I was six then went
To live elsewhere when I was eight years old.
For ages I remembered her faint scent
Of lavender, the way she'd never scold
No matter what I'd done, and most of all
The way her smile seemed, somehow, to enfold
My whole world like a warm, protective shawl.

I knew that I was safe when she was near,
She was so tall, so wide, so large, she would
Stand mountainous between me and my fear,
Yet oh, so gentle, and she understood
Every hope and dream I ever had.
She praised me lavishly when I was good,
But never punished me when I was bad.

Years later war broke out and I became
A soldier and was wounded while in France.
Back home in hospital, still very lame,
I realized suddenly that circumstance
Had brought me close to that small town where she
Was living still. And so I seized the chance
To write and ask if she could visit me.

She came. And I still vividly recall
The shock that I received when she appeared
That dark cold day. Huge grannie was so small!
A tiny, frail, old lady. It was weird.
She hobbled through the ward to where I lay
And drew quite close and, hesitating, peered.
And then she smiled: and love lit up the day.

Vernon Scannell

THE KRAKEN

Below the thunders of the upper deep;
Far, far beneath in the abysmal sea,
His ancient, dreamless, uninvaded sleep
The Kraken sleepeth: faintest sunlights flee
About his shadowy sides: above him swell
Huge sponges of millennial growth and height;
And far away into the sickly light,
From many a wondrous grot and secret cell
Unnumber'd and enormous polypi
Winnow with giant arms the slumbering green.
There hath he lain for ages and will lie
Battening upon huge seaworms in his sleep,
Until the latter fire shall heat the deep;
Then once by man and angels to be seen,
In roaring he shall rise and on the surface die.

Alfred Lord Tennyson

THE CAT AND THE MOON

The cat went here and there
And the moon spun round like a top,
And the nearest kin of the moon,
The creeping cat, looked up.
Black Minnaloushe stared at the moon,
For wander and wail as he would,
The pure cold light in the sky
Troubled his animal blood.
Minnaloushe runs in the grass
Lifting his delicate feet.
Do you dance, Minnaloushe, do you dance?
When two close kindred meet
What better than call a dance?
Maybe the moon may learn,
Tired of that courtly fashion,
A new dance turn.
Minnaloushe creeps through the grass
From moonlit place to place.
The sacred moon overhead
Has taken a new phase.
Does Minnaloushe know that his pupils
Will pass from change to change,
And that from round to crescent,
From crescent to round they range?
Minnaloushe creeps through the grass
Alone, important and wise,
And lifts to the changing moon
His changing eyes.

W B Yeats

GRADE FIVE *PROSE*

THE HITCHHIKER'S GUIDE TO THE GALAXY

"Ford," insisted Arthur, "I don't know if this sounds like a silly question, but what am I doing here?"

"Well you know that," said Ford. "I rescued you from the Earth."

"And what's happened to the Earth?"

"Ah. It's been demolished."

"Has it," said Arthur levelly.

"Yes. It just boiled away into space."

"Look," said Arthur, "I'm a bit upset about that."

Ford frowned to himself and seemed to roll the thought around his mind.

"Yes, I can understand that," he said at last.

"Understand that!" shouted Arthur. "Understand that!"

Ford sprang up.

"Keep looking at the book!" he hissed urgently.

"What?"

"*Don't Panic.*"

"I'm not panicking!"

"Yes you are."

"Alright so I'm panicking, what else is there to do?"

"You just come along with me and have a good time. The Galaxy's a fun place. You'll need to have this fish in your ear."

"I beg your pardon?" asked Arthur, rather politely he thought.

Ford was holding up a small glass jar which quite clearly had a small yellow fish wriggling around in it. Arthur blinked at him. He wished there was something simple and recognizable he could grasp hold of. He would have felt safe if alongside the Dentrassi underwear, the piles of Sqornshellous mattresses and the man from Betelgeuse holding up a small yellow fish and offering to put it in his ear he had been able to see just a small packet of corn flakes. But he couldn't, and he didn't feel safe.

Douglas Adams

HOW IT HAPPENED
(a short story from *Tales of Unease*)

"What a smash!" I said. "Good Lord, what an awful smash!"

He nodded his head, and even in the gloom I could see that he was smiling the gentle, wistful smile which I connected with him.

I was quite unable to move. Indeed, I had not any desire to try to move. But my senses were exceedingly alert. I saw the wreck of the motor lit up by the moving lanterns. I saw the little group of people and heard the hushed voices. There were the lodge-keeper and his wife, and one or two more. They were taking no notice of me, but were very busy round the car. Then suddenly I heard a cry of pain.

"The weight is on him. Lift it easy," cried a voice.

"It's only my leg!" said another one, which I recognised as Perkins's. "Where's master?" he cried.

"Here I am," I answered, but they did not seem to hear me. They were all bending over something which lay in front of the car.

Stanley laid his hand upon my shoulder, and his touch was inexpressibly soothing. I felt light and happy, in spite of all.

"No pain, of course?" said he.

"None," said I.

"There never is," said he.

And then suddenly a wave of amazement passed over me. Stanley! Stanley! Why, Stanley had surely died of enteric at Bloemfontein in the Boer War!

"Stanley!" I cried, and the words seemed to choke my throat – "Stanley, you are dead."

Sir Arthur Conan Doyle

ROSES FROM THE EARTH: THE BIOGRAPHY OF ANNE FRANK

Hours passed and they knew they were in Germany. Whenever the train stopped, a guard would open the door and throw in a bucket of beet marmalade and a few pieces of bread. They sometimes stopped for hours, and the guards outside would shout for them to surrender their valuables. A few handed over coins and jewellery that they had sewn into their clothes. The toilet pail was yanked out, emptied, and flung back in.

Anne, Margot, Peter and Judy sat together, talking quietly and occasionally climbing up on the bars to peep out of the window. A young man who was keeping watch stepped aside for them; he had been trying to determine where they were. "Anne was riding though the country of her birth," Rosa recalled, "but it might as well have been Brazil or Asia, for even when they were able to read the name of a station as it flitted by outside, the name meant nothing to us; the place was only a small village. All we did know was that we were headed east…we adults were silent. At most we would ask the children once again whether they still remembered the addresses, nothing more."

At night it was impossible to sleep. The jarring of the cattle-trucks, the stench and the fear kept them awake. Tempers frayed and people argued, shouted and sobbed. Lenie de Jong-van Naarden remembers how Edith tried to occupy herself: "Mrs Frank had smuggled out a pair of overalls and she sat by the light of the candle, ripping off the red patch. She must have thought that without that red patch, they wouldn't be able to see that we were convict prisoners…for her it was important and she got some satisfaction from doing it. Many people, among them the Frank girls, leaned against their father or mother, everyone was dead tired." In his memoir, Otto recalled the journey in just two sentences: "The awful transportation – three days locked in a cattle truck – was the last time I saw my family. Each of us tried to be as courageous as possible and not to let our heads drop."

The night of the third day, the train started to slow down.

Carol Ann Lee

THREE MEN IN A BOAT

I called for the cheeses, and took them away in a cab. It was a ramshackle affair, dragged along by a knock-kneed, broken-winded somnambulist, which his owner, in a moment of enthusiasm, during conversation, referred to as a horse. I put the cheeses on the top, and we started off at a shamble that would have done credit to the swiftest steam-roller ever built, and all went merry as a funeral bell, until we turned a corner. There, the wind carried a whiff from the cheeses full on our steed. It woke him up, and, with a snort of terror, he dashed off at three miles an hour. The wind still blew in his direction, and before we reached the end of the street he was laying himself out at the rate of nearly four miles an hour, leaving the cripples and stout old ladies simply nowhere.

It took two porters as well as the driver to hold him in at the station; and I do not think they would have done it, even then, had not one of the men had the presence of mind to put a handkerchief over his nose, and to light a bit of brown paper.

I took my ticket, and marched proudly up the platform, with my cheeses, the people falling back respectfully on either side. The train was crowded, and I had to get into a carriage where there were already seven other people. One crusty old gentleman objected, but I got in, notwithstanding; and, putting my cheeses upon the rack, squeezed down with a pleasant smile, and said it was a warm day. A few moments passed, and then the old gentleman began to fidget:

"Very close in here," he said.

"Quite oppressive," said the man next to him.

And then they both began sniffing, and, at the third sniff, they caught it right on the chest, and rose up without another word and went out.

Jerome K Jerome

THE LADY AND THE SQUIRE

"Say to yourself: 'I'm a girl'!" Tom told himself. "Walk the way a girl would walk." He had just taken his first – what he hoped was girl-like – step, when he felt a strange sensation behind that made him jump out of his skin. He turned to find the long guard peering down at him.

Of course! How could he have been so stupid as to imagine anyone would not see that he was a boy, dressed up in girl's clothes that were too big for him anyway? Tom's knees didn't exactly knock, but they certainly seemed to huddle together for comfort. He took a deep breath and was just about to do the only thing he could think of in the circumstances – i.e. head-butt the guard in the stomach – when he noticed that the man was not scowling at him. In fact he was smiling – and smiling in the most peculiar way.

"Hello, darling," the guard was saying, "I haven't seen you here before." And Tom suddenly realized – in one of those flashes of inspiration that come to us all occasionally – that the strange sensation that had made him jump out of his skin was the sensation of having his bottom pinched!

"Of all the cheek!" thought Tom indignantly.

"And what's your name, little darling?" asked the guard.

"Er…my name?" Tom's mind went blank. He couldn't think of a single girl's name.

"Oh, a right little shy one, eh?" smiled the guard.

"My name is… T… T…" It was no use, Tom just couldn't think of anything except Thomas and Timothy and Terence and Tancred and Talbot and Tristram and Titus and Toby!

"Tabitha?" enquired the guard helpfully.

"No!" said Tom, "I mean yes! Tabitha!"

"That's a nice name," said the guard.

"For goodness' sake! He's talking to me as if I were a five-year-old!" thought Tom, backing away from the overfriendly soldier.

"I'm off duty in a couple of hours," smiled the guard, as he cornered Tom against a pillar.

Terry Jones

THE GIFT OF THE MAGI
(a short story from *100 Selected Stories*)

Now, there were two possessions of the James Dillingham Youngs in which they both took a mighty pride. One was Jim's gold watch that had been his father's and his grandfather's. The other was Della's hair. Had the Queen of Sheba lived in the flat across the airshaft, Della would have let her hair hang out the window some day to dry just to depreciate Her Majesty's jewels and gifts. Had King Solomon been the janitor, with all his treasures piled up in the basement, Jim would have pulled out his watch every time he passed, just to see him pluck at his beard from envy.

So now Della's beautiful hair fell about her, rippling and shining like a cascade of brown waters. It reached below her knee and made itself almost a garment for her. And then she did it up again nervously and quickly. Once she faltered for a minute and stood still while a tear or two splashed on the worn red carpet.

On went her old brown jacket; on went her old brown hat. With a whirl of skirts and with the brilliant sparkle still in her eyes, she fluttered out of the door and down the stairs to the street.

Where she stopped the sign read: 'Mme. Sofronie. Hair Goods of All Kinds.' One flight up Della ran, and collected herself, panting. Madame, large, too white, chilly, hardly looked the 'Sofronie'.

"Will you buy my hair?" asked Della.

"I buy hair," said Madame. "Take yer hat off and let's have a sight at the looks of it."

Down rippled the brown cascade.

"Twenty dollars," said Madame, lifting the mass with a practised hand.

O Henry

WYRD SISTERS

Silence again filled the makeshift theatre except for the hesitant voices of the actors, who kept glancing at the bristling figure of Granny Weatherwax, and the sucking sounds of a couple of boiled humbugs being relentlessly churned from cheek to cheek.

Then Granny said, in a piercing voice that made one actor drop his wooden sword, "There's a man over on the side there whispering to them!"

"He's a prompter," said Magrat. "He tells them what to say."

"Don't they know?"

"I think they're forgetting," said Magrat sourly. "For some reason."

Granny nudged Nanny Ogg.

"What's going on now?" she said. "Why're all them kings and people up there?"

"It's a banquet, see," said Nanny Ogg authoritatively. "Because of the dead king, him in the boots, as was, only now if you look, you'll see he's pretending to be a soldier, and everyone's making speeches about how good he was and wondering who killed him."

"Are they?" said Granny, grimly. She cast her eyes along the cast, looking for the murderer.

She was making up her mind.

Then she stood up.

Her black shawl billowed around her like the wings of an avenging angel, come to rid the world of all that was foolishness and pretence and artifice and sham. She seemed somehow a lot bigger than normal. She pointed an angry finger at the guilty party.

"He done it!" she shouted triumphantly. "We all *seed* 'im! He done it with a dagger!"

Terry Pratchett

AROUND THE WORLD IN EIGHTY DAYS

"Five more minutes," said Andrew Stuart.

The five colleagues looked at each other. One may surmise that their hearts were beating slightly faster since the stake was a big one even for such bold gamblers! But they didn't want it to show, and followed Samuel Fallentin's suggestion that they sit down at a card-table.

"I wouldn't sell my £4,000 share in this bet," said Andrew Stuart, sitting down, "even for £3,999!"

The hands indicated 8.42 at this moment.

The players picked up the cards; but their eyes strayed to the clock every few seconds. One may safely say that however secure they felt, never had minutes seemed so long to them!

"Forty-three," said Flanagan, cutting the pack that Ralph had placed in front of him.

There came a moment of silence. The huge club room was quiet. But the hubbub of the crowd could be heard outside, dominated sometimes by shrill shouts. The pendulum of the clock beat every second with mathematical regularity. Each of the players counted the sexagesimal units reaching his ear.

"Eight forty-four!" said John Sullivan, in a voice where emotion could be heard, even though he tried to hide it.

Only a minute to go, and the bet was won. Stuart and his colleagues were not playing any more. They had laid their cards down. They were counting the seconds.

At the fortieth second, nothing. At the fiftieth, still nothing.

At the fifty-fifth, a sound like thunder could be heard outside, the sound of clapping, of hoorays, even of swear-words, spreading as a continuous roll.

The players got to their feet.

On the fifty-seventh second, the door of the drawing-room opened. Before the pendulum could beat the sixtieth second, Mr Phileas Fogg appeared, followed by a delirious crowd forcing its way into the Club. A calm voice was heard.

"Here I am, gentlemen."

Yes! Phileas Fogg in person.

Jules Verne

GRADE SIX –
BRONZE MEDAL *VERSE*

THE GREAT GALES
RAGE IN THE TREES

The great gales rage in the trees outside the window.
    The moon races
over mottled water meadows and in shadows
    and moonlight the surfaces
    of the nightmare stream glint
and shiver in the wind as winter
    shrieks in the chimney stack
and not even the far obedient star
    believes it can ever bring
    the summer back.
The dog whimpers. A door slams. The shutters
    clap and a sleeping child
    stirs with a haunted sigh
    as the storm mutters
and groans around this dreaming and lonely
    house. From tossing trees
    the torn boughs
hang swaying dislocated, and uneasily
    the wood fire gutters
    as hisses and spits
    of rain sputter and drip
    into tiny blazes. I watch
    the year turning
    and burning to ash
    once more, once more
and hear the breathtaking grave-haunting wolf
    of death at the door.

George Barker

SONG OF THE BATTERY HEN

We can't grumble about accommodation:
we have a new concrete floor that's
always dry, four walls that are
painted white, and a sheet-iron roof
the rain drums on. A fan blows warm air
beneath our feet to disperse the smell
of chicken-shit and, on dull days,
fluorescent lighting sees us.

You can tell me: if you come by
the North door, I am in the twelfth pen
on the left-hand side of the third row
from the floor; and in that pen
I am usually the middle one of three.
But, even without directions, you'd
discover me. I have the same orange-
red comb, yellow beak and auburn
feathers, but as the door opens and you
hear above the electric fan a kind of
one-word wail, I am the one
who sounds loudest in my head.

Listen. Outside this house there's an
orchard with small moss-green apple
trees; beyond that, two fields of
cabbages; then, on the far side of
the road, a broiler house. Listen:
one cockerel grows out of there, as
tall and proud as the first hour of sun.
Sometimes I stop calling with the others
to listen, and wonder if he hears me.

The next time you come here, look for me.
Notice the way I sound inside my head.
God made us all quite differently,
and blessed us with this expensive home.

Edwin Brock

MID-TERM BREAK

I sat all morning in the college sick bay,
Counting bells knelling classes to a close.
At two o'clock our neighbours drove me home.

In the porch I met my father crying –
He had always taken funerals in his stride –
And Big Jim Evans saying it was a hard blow.

The baby cooed and laughed and rocked the pram
When I came in, and I was embarrassed
By old men standing up to shake my hand

And tell me they were 'sorry for my trouble'.
Whispers informed strangers I was the eldest,
Away at school, as my mother held my hand

In hers and coughed out angry tearless sighs.
At ten o'clock the ambulance arrived
With the corpse, stanched and bandaged by the nurses.

Next morning I went up into the room. Snowdrops
And candles soothed the bedside; I saw him
For the first time in six weeks. Paler now,

Wearing a poppy bruise on his left temple,
He lay in the four foot box as in his cot.
No gaudy scars, the bumper knocked him clear.

A four foot box, a foot for every year.

Seamus Heaney

ANY PRINCE TO ANY PRINCESS

August is coming
and the goose, I'm afraid,
is getting fat.
There have been
no golden eggs for some months now.
Straw has fallen well below market price
despite my frantic spinning
and the sedge is,
as you rightly point out,
withered.

I can't imagine how the pea
got under your mattress. I apologize
humbly. The chambermaid has, of course,
been sacked. As has the frog footman.
I understand that, during my recent fact-finding tour of the
        Golden River,
despite your nightly unavailing efforts,
he remained obstinately
froggish.

I hope that the Three Wishes granted by the General
        Assembly
will go some way towards redressing
this unfortunate recent sequence of events.
The fall in output from the shoe-factory, for example:
no one could have foreseen the work-to-rule
by the National Union of Elves. Not to mention the fact
that the court has been fast asleep
for the last six and a half years.

The matter of the poisoned apple has been taken up
by the Board of Trade: I think I can assure you
the incident will not be
repeated.

I can quite understand, in the circumstances,
your reluctance to let down
your golden tresses. However
I feel I must point out
that the weather isn't getting any better
and I already have a nasty chill
from waiting at the base
of the White Tower. You must see the absurdity of the
     situation.
Some of the courtiers are beginning to talk,
not to mention the humble villagers.
It's been three weeks now, and not even
a word.

Princess,
a cold, black wind
howls through our empty palace.
Dead leaves litter the bedchamber;
the mirror on the wall hasn't said a thing
since you left. I can only ask,
bearing all this in mind,
that you think again,

let down your hair,

reconsider.

Adrian Henri

BIRTH OF THE FOAL

As May was opening the rosebuds,
elder and lilac beginning to bloom,
it was time for the mare to foal.
She'd rest herself, or hobble lazily

after the boy who sang as he led her
to pasture, wading through the meadowflowers.
They wandered back at dusk, bone-tired,
the moon perched on a blue shoulder of sky.

Then the mare lay down,
sweating and trembling, on her straw in the stable.
The drowsy, heavy-bellied cows
surrounded her, waiting, watching, snuffing.

Later, when even the hay slept
and the shaft of the Plough pointed south,
the foal was born. Hours the mare
spent licking the foal with its glue-blind eyes.

And the foal slept at her side,
a heap of feathers ripped from a bed.
Straw never spread as soft as this.
Milk or snow never slept like a foal.

Dawn bounced up in a bright red hat,
waved at the world and skipped away.
Up staggered the foal,
its hooves were jelly-knots of foam.

Then day sniffed with its blue nose
through the open stable window, and found them –
the foal nuzzling its mother,
velvet fumbling for her milk.

Then all the trees were talking at once,
chickens scrabbled in the yard,
like golden flowers
envy withered the last stars.

Ferenc Juhász
From the Hungarian (trans. David Wevill)

TO PAINT THE PORTRAIT OF A BIRD

To Elsa Henriquez

First paint a cage
with an open door
then paint
something pretty
something simple
something beautiful
something useful…
for the bird
then place the canvas against a tree
in a garden
in a wood
or in a forest
hide behind the tree
without speaking
without moving…
Sometimes the bird comes quickly
but he can just as well spend long years
before deciding
Don't get discouraged
wait
wait years if necessary
the swiftness or slowness of the coming

of the bird having no rapport
with the success of the picture
When the bird comes
if he comes
observe the most profound silence
wait till the bird enters the cage
and when he has entered
gently close the door with a brush
then
paint out all the bars one by one
taking care not to touch any of the feathers of the bird
Then paint the portrait of the tree
choosing the most beautiful of its branches
for the bird
paint also the green foliage and the wind's freshness
the dust of the sun
and the noise of the insects in the summer heat
and then wait for the bird to decide to sing
If the bird doesn't sing
it's a bad sign
a sign that the painting is bad
but if he sings it's a good sign
a sign that you can sign
So then so very gently you pull out
one of the feathers of the bird
and you write your name in the corner of the picture.

Jacques Prévert
(trans. Lawrence Ferlinghetti)

CINDERELLA

My step-sisters are willing
to cut off their toes for him.

What would I do for those days
when I played alone
in the hazel tree over my mother's grave?

I would go backwards if I could
and stay in that moment when the doves
fluttered down with the golden gown.

But everything has changed.
I trace his form in the ashes,
and then sweep it away before they see.

He's been on parade with that shoe.
All Prince, with heralds and entourage,
they come trumpeting through the village.

If he found me, would he recognise me,
my face, after mistaking their feet for mine?
I want to crawl away

into my pigeon house, my pear tree.
The world is too large, bright like a ballroom
and then suddenly dark.

Mother, no one prepared me for this –
for the soft heat of a man's neck when he dances
or the thickness of his arms.

Gwen Strauss

THE SUNBATHER

I shield my face. My eyes are closed. I spin
With nearing sleep. I am dissolved within
Myself, and softened like a ripening fruit.
I swing in a red-hazy void, I sway
With tides of blind heat. From a far-off sphere,
Like scratchings on a pillow, voices I hear
And thundering waves and thuds of passing feet;
For there, out there beyond me, lads and girls
In dazzling colours and with gleaming skin
Through sands of gold and surfs of opal run;
They dive beneath the long green claw which curls
Above them; on the white comber they shoot
Shoreward; many in a slow spiral melt
Like me into oblivion under the sun.

John Thompson

GRADE SIX –
BRONZE MEDAL *PROSE*

PRIDE AND PREJUDICE

"My dear Jane, make haste and hurry down. He is come – Mr Bingley is come. – He is, indeed. Make haste, make haste. Here, Sarah, come to Miss Bennet this moment, and help her on with her gown. Never mind Miss Lizzy's hair."

"We will be down as soon as we can," said Jane; "but I dare say Kitty is forwarder than either of us, for she went up stairs half an hour ago."

"Oh! hang Kitty! what has she to do with it? Come be quick, be quick! where is your sash my dear?"

But when her mother was gone, Jane would not be prevailed on to go down without one of her sisters.

The same anxiety to get them by themselves, was visible again in the evening. After tea, Mr Bennet retired to the library, as was his custom, and Mary went up stairs to her instrument. Two obstacles of the five being thus removed, Mrs Bennet sat looking and winking at Elizabeth and Catherine for a considerable time, without making any impression on them. Elizabeth would not observe her; and when at last Kitty did, she very innocently said, "What is the matter mamma? What do you keep winking at me for? What am I to do?"

"Nothing child, nothing. I did not wink at you." She then sat still five minutes longer; but unable to waste such a precious occasion, she suddenly got up, and saying to Kitty,

"Come here, my love, I want to speak to you," took her out of the room. Jane instantly gave a look at Elizabeth, which spoke her distress at such premeditation, and her intreaty that *she* would not give into it. In a few minutes, Mrs Bennet half opened the door and called out,

"Lizzy, my dear, I want to speak with you."

Jane Austen

HARD TIMES

"Girl number twenty," said Mr Gradgrind, squarely pointing with his square forefinger, "I don't know that girl. Who is that girl?"

"Sissy Jupe, Sir," explained number twenty, blushing, standing up, and curtseying.

"Sissy is not a name," said Mr Gradgrind. "Don't call yourself Sissy. Call yourself Cecilia."

"It's father as calls me Sissy, Sir," returned the young girl in a trembling voice, and with another curtsey.

"Then he has no business to do it," said Mr Gradgrind. "Tell him he mustn't. Cecilia Jupe. Let me see. What is your father?"

"He belongs to the horse-riding, if you please, Sir."

Mr Gradgrind frowned, and waved off the objectionable calling with his hand.

"We don't want to know anything about that, here. You mustn't tell us about that, here. Your father breaks horses, don't he?"

"If you please, Sir, when they can get any to break, they do break horses in the ring, Sir."

"You mustn't tell us about the ring, here. Very well, then. Describe your father as a horsebreaker. He doctors sick horses, I dare say?"

"Oh yes, Sir."

"Very well, then. He is a veterinary surgeon, a farrier, and horsebreaker. Give me your definition of a horse."

(Sissy Jupe thrown into the greatest alarm by this demand.)

"Girl number twenty unable to define a horse!" said Mr Gradgrind, for the general behoof of all the little pitchers. "Girl number twenty possessed of no facts, in reference to one of the commonest animals! Some boy's definition of a horse. Bitzer, yours."

"Quadruped. Graminivorous. Forty teeth, namely twenty-four grinders, four eye-teeth, and twelve incisive. Sheds coat in the spring; in marshy countries, sheds hoofs, too. Hoofs hard, but requiring to be shod with iron. Age known by marks in mouth." Thus (and much more) Bitzer.

"Now girl number twenty," said Mr Gradgrind. "You know what a horse is."

Charles Dickens

REBECCA

I heard a step behind me and turning round I saw Mrs Danvers. I shall never forget the expression on her face. Triumphant, gloating, excited in a strange unhealthy way. I felt very frightened.

"Is anything the matter, Madam?" she said.

I tried to smile at her, and could not. I tried to speak.

"Are you feeling unwell?" she said, coming nearer to me, speaking very softly. I backed away from her. I believe if she had come any closer to me I should have fainted. I felt her breath on my face.

"I'm all right, Mrs Danvers," I said, after a moment, "I did not expect to see you. The fact is, I was looking up at the windows from the lawn. I noticed one of the shutters was not quite closed. I came up to see if I could fasten it."

"I will fasten it," she said, and she went silently across the room and clamped back the shutter. The daylight had gone. The room looked unreal again in the false yellow light. Unreal and ghastly.

Mrs Danvers came back and stood beside me. She smiled, and her manner, instead of being still and unbending as it usually was, became startlingly familiar, fawning even.

"Why did you tell me the shutter was open?" she asked. "I closed it before I left the room. You opened it yourself, didn't you, now? You wanted to see the room. Why have you never asked me to show it to you before? I was ready to show it to you every day. You had only to ask me."

I wanted to run away, but I could not move.

Daphne du Maurier

CHOCOLAT

The door is unlocked. I can hardly believe my luck. It shows her confidence, her insolent belief that no-one can withstand her. I discard the thick screwdriver with which I would have jimmied the door, and take up the heavy piece of wood – part of a lintel, *père*, that fell during the war – in both hands. The door opens into silence. Another of her red sachets swings above the doorway; I pull it down and drop it contemptuously onto the floor. For a time I am disoriented. The place has changed since it was a bakery, and in any case I am less familiar with the back part of the shop. Only a very faint reflection of light gleams from the tiled surfaces, and I am glad I thought to bring a torch. I switch it on now, and for a moment I am almost blinded by the whiteness of the enamelled surfaces, the tops, the sinks, the old ovens all shining with a moony glow in the torch's narrow beam. There are no chocolates to be seen. Of course. This is only the preparation area. I am not sure why I am surprised that the place is so clean; I imagined her a slattern, leaving pans unwashed and plates stacked in the sink and long black hairs in the cake mixture. Instead she is scrupulously tidy; rows of pans arranged on the shelves in order of size, copper with copper, enamel with enamel, porcelain bowls to hand and utensils – spoons, skillets – hanging from the whitewashed walls. On the scarred old table several stone bread pans are standing. In the centre, a vase with shaggy yellow dahlias cast a shock of shadows before them. For some reason the flowers enrage me. What right has she to flowers, when Armande Voizin lies dead? The pig inside me tips the flowers onto the table, grinning. I let him have his way. I need his ferocity for the task in hand.

Joanne Harris

THE STRANGE CASE OF DR JEKYLL AND MR HYDE

Some two months before the murder of Sir Danvers, I had been out for one of my adventures, had returned at a late hour, and woke the next day in bed with somewhat odd sensations. It was in vain I looked about me; in vain I saw the decent furniture and tall proportions of my room in the square; in vain that I recognized the pattern of the bed curtains and the design of the mahogany frame; something still kept insisting that I was not where I was, that I had not wakened where I seemed to be, but in the little room in Soho where I was accustomed to sleep in the body of Edward Hyde. I smiled to myself, and, in my psychological way, began lazily to inquire into the elements of this illusion, occasionally, even as I did so, dropping back into a comfortable morning doze. I was still so engaged when, in one of my more wakeful moments, my eye fell upon my hand. Now, the hand of Henry Jekyll (as you have often remarked) was professional in shape and size; it was large, firm, white and comely. But the hand which I now saw, clearly enough in the yellow light of a mid-London morning, lying half shut on the bed-clothes, was lean, corded, knuckly, of a dusky pallor, and thickly shaded with a swart growth of hair. It was the hand of Edward Hyde.

I must have stared upon it for near half a minute, sunk as I was in the mere stupidity of wonder, before terror woke up in my breast as sudden and startling as the crash of cymbals; and bounding from my bed, I rushed to the mirror. At the sight that met my eyes, my blood was changed into something exquisitely thin and icy. Yes, I had gone to bed Henry Jekyll, I had awakened Edward Hyde.

Robert Louis Stevenson

THE FELLOWSHIP OF THE RING

"The Ring! The Ring!" they cried with deadly voices; and immediately their leader urged his horse forward into the water, followed closely by two others.

"By Elbereth and Lúthien the Fair," said Frodo with a last effort, lifting up his sword, "you shall have neither the Ring nor me!"

Then the leader, who was now half across the Ford, stood up menacing in his stirrups, and raised up his hand. Frodo was stricken dumb. He felt his tongue cleave to his mouth, and his heart labouring. His sword broke and fell out of his shaking hand. The elf-horse reared and snorted. The foremost of the black horses had almost set foot upon the shore.

At that moment there came a roaring and a rushing: a noise of loud waters rolling many stones. Dimly Frodo saw the river below him rise, and down along its course there came a plumed cavalry of waves. White flames seemed to Frodo to flicker on their crests and he half fancied that he saw amid the water white riders upon white horses with frothing manes. The three Riders that were still in the midst of the Ford were overwhelmed: they disappeared, buried suddenly under angry foam. Those that were behind drew back in dismay.

With his last failing senses Frodo heard cries, and it seemed to him that he saw, beyond the Riders that hesitated on the shore, a shining figure of white light; and behind it ran small shadowy forms waving flames, that flared red in the grey mist that was falling over the world.

J R R Tolkien

THE NIGHTINGALE AND THE ROSE
(from *The Happy Prince and Other Stories*)

She sang first of the birth of love in the heart of a boy and a girl. And on the topmost spray of the Rose-tree there blossomed a marvellous rose, petal following petal, as song followed song. Pale was it, at first, as the mist that hangs over the river – pale as the feet of the morning, and silver as the wings of the dawn. As the shadow of a rose in a mirror of silver, as the shadow of a rose in a water-pool, so was the rose that blossomed on the topmost spray of the Tree.

But the Tree cried to the Nightingale to press closer against the thorn. "Press closer, little Nightingale," cried the Tree, "or the Day will come before the rose is finished."

So the Nightingale pressed closer against the thorn, and louder and louder grew her song, for she sang of the birth of passion in the soul of a man and a maid.

And a delicate flush of pink came into the leaves of the rose, like the flush in the face of the bridegroom when he kisses the lips of the bride. But the thorn had not yet reached her heart, so the rose's heart remained white, for only a Nightingale's heart's-blood can crimson the heart of a rose.

And the Tree cried to the Nightingale to press closer against the thorn. "Press closer, little Nightingale," cried the Tree, "or the Day will come before the rose is finished."

So the Nightingale pressed closer against the thorn, and the thorn touched her heart, and a fierce pang of pain shot through her. Bitter, bitter was the pain, and wilder and wilder grew her song, for she sang of the Love that is perfected by Death, of the Love that dies not in the tomb.

And the marvellous rose became crimson, like the rose of the eastern sky. Crimson was the girdle of petals, and crimson as a ruby was the heart.

But the Nightingale's voice grew fainter, and her little wings began to beat, and a film came over her eyes. Fainter and fainter grew her song, and she felt something choking her in her throat.

Oscar Wilde

FLUSH

At last the longed-for moment would come. She thrust her papers aside, clapped a hat on her head, took her umbrella and set off for a walk across the fields with her dogs. Spaniels are by nature sympathetic; Flush, as his story proves, had an even excessive appreciation of human emotions. The sight of his dear mistress snuffing the fresh air at last, letting it ruffle her white hair and redden the natural freshness of her face, while the lines on her huge brow smoothed themselves out, excited him to gambols whose wildness was half sympathy with her own delight. As she strode through the long grass, so he leapt hither and thither, parting its green curtain. The cool globes of dew or rain broke in showers of iridescent spray about his nose; the earth, here hard, here soft, here hot, here cold, stung, teased and tickled the soft pads of his feet. Then what a variety of smells interwoven in subtlest combination thrilled his nostrils; strong smells of earth, sweet smells of flowers; nameless smells of leaf and bramble; sour smells as they crossed the road; pungent smells as they entered bean-fields. But suddenly down the wind came tearing a smell sharper, stronger, more lacerating than any—a smell that ripped across his brain stirring a thousand instincts, releasing a million memories—the smell of hare, the smell of fox. Off he flashed like a fish drawn in a rush through water further and further. He forgot his mistress; he forgot all human kind. He heard dark men cry "Span! Span!" He heard whips crack. He raced; he rushed. At last he stopped bewildered; the incantation faded; very slowly, wagging his tail sheepishly, he trotted back across the fields to where Miss Mitford stood shouting "Flush! Flush! Flush!" and waving her umbrella.

Virginia Woolf

GRADE SEVEN –
SILVER MEDAL *VERSE*

STILL I RISE

You may write me down in history
With your bitter, twisted lies,
You may trod me in the very dirt
But still, like dust, I'll rise.

Does my sassiness upset you?
Why are you beset with gloom?
'Cause I walk like I've got oil wells
Pumping in my living room.

Just like moons and like suns,
With the certainty of tides,
Just like hopes springing high,
Still I'll rise.

Did you want to see me broken?
Bowed head and lowered eyes?
Shoulders falling down like teardrops,
Weakened by my soulful cries?

Does my haughtiness offend you?
Don't you take it awful hard
'Cause I laugh like I've got gold mines
Diggin' in my own backyard.

You may shoot me with your words,
You may cut me with your eyes,
You may kill me with your hatefulness,
But still, like air, I'll rise.

Does my sexiness upset you?
Does it come as a surprise
That I dance like I've got diamonds
At the meeting of my thighs?

Out of the huts of history's shame
I rise
Up from a past that's rooted in pain
I rise
I'm a black ocean, leaping and wide,
Welling and swelling I bear in the tide.

Leaving behind nights of terror and fear
I rise
Into a daybreak that's wondrously clear
I rise
Bringing the gifts that my ancestors gave,
I am the dream and the hope of the slave.
I rise
I rise
I rise.

Maya Angelou

IF I COULD TELL YOU

Time will say nothing but I told you so,
Time only knows the price we have to pay;
If I could tell you I would let you know.

If we should weep when clowns put on their show,
If we should stumble when musicians play,
Time will say nothing but I told you so.

There are no fortunes to be told, although,
Because I love you more than I can say,
If I could tell you I would let you know.

The winds must come from somewhere when they blow,
There must be reasons why the leaves decay;
Time will say nothing but I told you so.

Perhaps the roses really want to grow,
The vision seriously intends to stay;
If I could tell you I would let you know.

Suppose the lions all get up and go,
And all the brooks and soldiers run away;
Will Time say nothing but I told you so?
If I could tell you I would let you know.

W H Auden

TARANTELLA

Do you remember an Inn,
Miranda?
Do you remember an Inn?
And the tedding and the spreading
Of the straw for a bedding,
And the fleas that tease in the High Pyrenees,
And the wine that tasted of the tar,
And the cheers and the jeers of the young muleteers
(Under the vine of the dark verandah)?
Do you remember an Inn, Miranda,
Do you remember an Inn?
And the cheers and the jeers of the young muleteers
Who hadn't got a penny,
And who weren't paying any,
And the hammer at the doors and the Din?

And the Hip! Hop! Hap!
Of the clap
Of the hands to the twirl and the swirl
Of the girl gone chancing,
Glancing,
Dancing,

Backing and advancing,
Snapping of the clapper to the spin
Out and in—
And the Ting, Tong, Tang of the Guitar!
Do you remember an Inn,
Miranda?
Do you remember an Inn?

Never more,
Miranda,
Never more.
Only the high peaks hoar:
And Aragon a torrent at the door.
No sound
In the walls of the Halls where falls
The tread
Of the feet of the dead to the ground,
No sound:
But the boom
Of the far Waterfall like Doom.

Hilaire Belloc

OLD LADY

Miss Mahaffey was her name
all faded lace and silver hair
her face already a skull upon the pillow
lit eerily at night from the streetlight
beaming at the mouth of the narrow lane
below the dull distempered walls of her ward

a frail rainbow fall of silk
faintly smudged at the edges
was little Miss Mahaffey
shrunken and sunken into yesterday
fragile shadow on parched landscape
fingers stirring like limp mice
twitching on the winding shrouds of sheets
maiden lady clinging to grace and dignity
gently lying in her perpetual twilight
not bothering the hurrying nurses for a drop of water
brought by life's meaner barbarities to this
wrinkled and shriveled up in a crisp bed
coughing up phlegm and speckled blood
being incontinent in the night

a genteel ghost whispering words of no complaint
patient as the plot of earth marked out
to receive her few fish-thin bones
all beauty safely behind her
save briefly when she opened her eyes
to the night nurse bending over her
and murmured "sorry".

Christy Brown

DEPORTATION

They have not been kind here. Now I must leave,
the words I've learned for supplication,
gratitude, will go unused. Love is a look
in the eyes in any language, but not here,
not this year. They have not been welcoming.

I used to think the world was where we lived
in space, one country shining in big dark.
I saw a photograph when I was small.

Now I am *Alien*. Where I come from there are few jobs,
the young are sullen and do not dream. My lover
bears our child and I was to work here, find
a home. In twenty years we would say This is you
when you were a baby, when the plum tree was a shoot...

We will tire each other out, making our homes
in one another's arms. We are not strong enough.

They are polite, recite official jargon endlessly.
Form F. Room 12. Box 6. I have felt less small
below mountains disappearing into cloud
than entering the Building of Exile. Hearse taxis
crawl the drizzling streets towards the terminal.

I am no one special. An ocean parts me from my love.

Go back. She will embrace me, ask what it was like.
Return. One thing – there was a space to write
the colour of her eyes. They have an apple here,
a bitter-sweet, which matches them exactly. Dearest,
without you I am nowhere. It was cold.

Carol Ann Duffy

TITANIA TO BOTTOM

You had all the best lines. I
Was the butt, too immortal
To be taken seriously. I don't grudge you
That understated donkey dignity.
It belongs to your condition. Only,
Privately, you should know my passion
Wasn't the hallucination they imagined,
Meddling king and sniggering fairy.

You, Bottom, are what I love. That nose,
Supple, aware; that muzzle, planted out
With stiff, scratchable hairs; those ears,
Lofty as bulrushes, smelling of hay harvest,
Twitching to each subtle electric
Flutter of the brain! Oberon's loving
Was like eating myself – appropriate,
Tasteless, rather debilitating.

But holding you I held the whole
Perishable world, rainfall and nightjar,
Tides, excrement, dandelions, the first foot,
The last pint, high blood pressure, accident, prose.

The sad mechanical drone of enchantment
Finished my dream. I knew what was proper,
Reverted to fairyland's style.

But Bottom, Bottom,
How I shook to the shuffle of your mortal heart.

U A Fanthorpe

THE MEETING PLACE
(after Rubens: *The Adoration of the Magi* 1634)

It was the arrival of the kings
that caught us unawares;
we'd looked in on the woman in the barn,
curiosity you could call it,
something to do on a cold winter's night;
we'd wished her well –
that was the best we could do, she was in pain,
and the next thing we knew
she was lying on the straw
– the little there was of it –
and there was this baby in her arms.

It was, as I say, the kings
that caught us unawares...
Women have babies every other day,
not that we are there –
let's call it a common occurrence though,
giving birth. But kings
appearing in a stable with a
'Is this the place?' and kneeling,
each with his gift held out towards the child!

They didn't even notice us.
Their robes trailed on the floor,
rich, lined robes that money couldn't buy.
What must this child be
to bring kings from distant lands
with costly incense and gold?
What could a tiny baby make of that?

And what were we to make of
was it angels falling through the air,
entwined and falling as if from the rafters
to where the gaze of the kings met the child's
        – assuming the child could see?

What would the mother do with the gifts?
What would become of the child?
And we'll never admit there are angels

or that somewhere between
one man's eyes and another's
is a holy place, a space where a king could be
at one with a naked child,
at one with an astonished soldier.

Christopher Pilling

THE HERO

'Jack fell as he'd have wished,' the Mother said,
And folded up the letter that she'd read.
'The Colonel writes so nicely.' Something broke
In the tired voice that quavered to a choke.
She half looked up. 'We mothers are so proud
Of our dead soldiers.' Then her face was bowed.

Quietly the Brother Officer went out.
He'd told the poor old dear some gallant lies
That she would nourish all her days, no doubt.
For while he coughed and mumbled, her weak eyes
Had shone with gentle triumph, brimmed with joy,
Because he'd been so brave, her glorious boy.

He thought how 'Jack', cold-footed, useless swine,
Had panicked down the trench that night the mine
Went up at Wicked Corner; how he'd tried
To get sent home, and how, at last, he died,
Blown to small bits. And no one seemed to care
Except that lonely woman with white hair.

Siegfried Sassoon

GRADE SEVEN –
SILVER MEDAL *PROSE*

NO BED FOR BACON

Cardinal Wolsey, seeing the group conversing so amiably and judging that the moment was ripe, hurried over and drew Shakespeare aside.

"Master Will," he said, "I want to be a ghost."

Shakespeare looked at him evilly.

On their right an epidemic of hammering had broken out. On their left a great deal of hoisting, whoa-ing, steadying and 'there-lads' was going on. Cardinal Wolsey felt that perhaps he had not made himself clear.

"A ghost," he repeated.

"A ghost," said Shakespeare, looking at him with hate. "You are going the right way about it."

Cardinal Wolsey backed. Perhaps he had not chosen the right moment.

"You misunderstand me," he said. "I speak of a stage ghost, who talks most chillingly, a perturbed spirit who walks at midnight and urges his son to avenge him."

"What for?" asked Shakespeare impatiently.

Cardinal Wolsey was confused. "I had not thought so far," he confessed. "I am not a Dekker." He caught sight of Master Will's face. "A Shakespeare," he amended hastily. "You could write a fine speech for a ghost," he tempted.

"Indeed," said Shakespeare.

"And I," said Cardinal Wolsey, feeling he might be fighting a losing battle, "can groan most horrid."

He groaned.

"Will," shouted Burbage. "Stop making those noises. I have an opening on my hands at four o'clock, I have a theatre to complete half an hour before, and I have your guests to get rid of at once…"

"My guests," said Shakespeare, furious.

The rest of the speech was lost in a crash. The beam had stopped steadying and whoa-ing, but it had come down. It had come down with a rush that had caught a swinging door and neatly penned Master Bacon into an unswept and very small corner. To get him out they would have to unhinge the door and carry away the beam, an operation for which, as Burbage pointed out, there was simply no time at the moment.

"Take it easy, Master Bacon," advised Shakespeare. "Stop shouting. I promise we shall have you out in time for the performance."

"And anyway," said Sidney, soothingly, "you can see quite well from there." He stood on his toes and craned.

"In the meantime," said Cardinal Wolsey, helpfully, "I will fetch you some ale."

"Ale," said Burbage dangerously.

Caryl Brahms & S J Simon

YEAR OF WONDERS

Mompellion was speaking to Aphra, his voice a low and soothing hum. I could not hear the words he said, but slowly the tension seemed to go out of her body, and as he eased his grip, I could see her shoulders heave with sobbing. Elinor was stroking Aphra's face with her left hand, while with her right she reached up to take the knife.

It might have been all right; it might have ended there. But the rector's arms, so tight upon Aphra, also encircled the remains of Faith's corpse. The pressure of that grip proved too much for the fragile bones. I heard the snap: a dry sound like a chicken's wishbone breaking. The little skull popped free of the spine and fell to the grass, where it rolled back and forth, the empty eyeholes staring.

I turned away in revulsion, and so I never saw exactly how it was that Aphra, wild in her new frenzy, landed her blows as she did. I know that it was an instant's work, merely. An instant's work, to take two lives and leave another ruined.

The wound on Elinor's neck was a wide, curved thing. For a second it was just a thin red line, upturned like a smile. But then the blood began spurting in bright bursts, streaking her white dress red. She crumpled on the ground, where the scattered flowers she had carried received her like a bier.

Aphra had turned the knife on herself and sunk it to the hilt, deep into her chest. Yet somehow she staggered, upright still, the uncanny strength of the lunatic keeping her on her feet. She lurched to where her baby's skull lay and then dropped to her knees, reached down, and with the most exquisite tenderness, gathered it up in her two hands and pressed it to her lips.

Geraldine Brooks

GIRL WITH A PEARL EARRING

As the house grew still, I remained in my chair. It was easier to sit there than do what I had to do. When I could not delay any longer, I got up and first peeked at the painting. All I could really see now was the great hole where the earring should go, which I would have to fill.

I took up my candle, found the mirror in the storeroom, and climbed to the attic. I propped the mirror against the wall on the grinding table and set the candle next to it. I got out my needlecase and, choosing the thinnest needle, set the tip in the flame of the candle. Then I opened the bottle of clove oil, expecting it to smell foul, of mould or rotting leaves, as remedies often do. Instead it was sweet and strange, like honeycakes left out in the sun. It was from far away, from places Frans might get to on his ships. I shook a few drops on to a rag, and swabbed my left earlobe. The apothecary was right – when I touched the lobe a few minutes later it felt as if I had been out in the cold without wrapping a shawl around my ears.

I took the needle out of the flame and let the glowing red tip change to dull orange and then to black. When I leaned towards the mirror I gazed at myself for a moment. My eyes were full of liquid in the candlelight, glittering with fear.

Do this quickly, I thought. It will not help to delay.

I pulled the earlobe taut and in one movement pushed the needle through my flesh.

Just before I fainted I thought, I have always wanted to wear pearls.

Tracy Chevalier

THE HOUSE BY THE DVINA

Dedushka looked tired. From the time he had returned from prison, he was kept busy in the hospital working late into the evening, and that day had not been different from the others. Now, enjoying the tranquility of the surrounding scene, he was quietly talking to Babushka. Marga was engaged on some embroidery with happy concentration. I joined Seryozha and Marina leaning against the railings and stood with them watching the progress of a small boat rowing across the river.

The peace was suddenly shattered by the resonant ringing of the front-door bell, Marga, dropping her sewing, rushed through the ballroom to the hall and opened the door.

Two men, in plain clothes, but armed, entered the hall. They demanded to see Dedushka and when he came forward they explained to him in courteous tones that they had been ordered to take him to a nearby prison, from where he would be sent into exile. It would be necessary, they continued in dispassionate tones, for Dedushka to pack the clothing he required, but the packing had to be done quickly as they had no time to waste.

Stunned, unable to think clearly, we all ran around gathering together Dedushka's belongings. Throughout the stress and anguish, only Dedushka himself remained calm. He helped Babushka, who could not contain her tears, to pack the old Gladstone bag with his clothes, a small Bible, and the medical instruments he thought he would require.

In the hall where the men were waiting, he blessed and kissed Babushka and in the same way said his goodbyes to us all, at times even passing a little joke. He then went to the nursery to embrace Father, and finally, turning to the men, said, "I'm ready, friends – let us go."

Ghermosha and I ran to the nursery window. We saw the three of them walking in the middle of the road, Dedushka carrying his bag, striding firmly, towering above the men either side of him.

That was my last glimpse of Dedushka. I never saw him again.

Eugenie Fraser

THE GLASS PALACE

The chamber was very large and its walls and columns were tiled with thousands of shards of glass. Oil lamps flared in sconces, and the whole room seemed to be aflame, every surface shimmering with sparks of golden light. The hall was filled with a busy noise, a workmanlike hum of cutting and chopping, of breaking wood and shattering glass. Everywhere people were intently at work, men and women, armed with axes and das; they were hacking at gem-studded *Ook* offering boxes; digging patterned gemstones from the marbled floor; using fish-hooks to pry the ivory inlays from lacquered sadaik chests. Armed with a rock, a girl was knocking the ornamental frets out of a crocodile-shaped zither; a man was using a meat cleaver to scrape the gilt from the neck of a *saung-gak* harp and a woman was chiselling furiously at the ruby eyes of a bronze *chinthe* lion. They came to a door that led to a candlelit anteroom. There was a woman inside, standing by the latticed window in the far corner.

Ma Cho gasped. 'Queen Supayalat!'

The Queen was screaming, shaking her fist. "Get out of here. Get out." Her face was red, mottled with rage, her fury caused as much by her own impotence as by the presence of the mob in the palace. A day before, she could have had a commoner imprisoned for so much as looking her directly in the face. Today all the city's scum had come surging into the palace and she was powerless to act against them. But the Queen was neither cowed nor afraid, not in the least. Ma Cho fell to the floor, her hands clasped over her head in a reverential *shiko*.

Amitav Ghosh

WHEN WE WERE ORPHANS

"From here, we'll go on foot," he said to me. "I know a good short cut. It'll be much quicker."

This made perfectly good sense. I knew from experience how the little streets off Nanking Road could become so clogged with people that a carriage or motor car would often not move for five, even ten minutes at a time. I thus allowed him to help me down from the carriage with no argument. But it was then, I recall, that I had my first presentiment that something was wrong. Perhaps it was something in Uncle Philip's touch as he handed me down; perhaps there was something else in his manner. But then he smiled and made some remark I did not catch in the noise around us. He pointed towards a nearby alley and I stayed close behind him as we pushed our way through the good-humoured throng. We moved from bright sun to shade, and then he stopped and turned to me, right there in the midst of the jostling crowd. Placing a hand on my shoulder, he asked:

"Christopher, do you know where we are now? Can you guess?"

I looked around me. Then pointing towards a stone arch under which crowds were pressing around the vegetable stalls, I replied: "Yes. That's Kiukiang Road through there."

"Ah. So you know exactly where we are." He gave an odd laugh. "You know your way around here very well."

I nodded and waited, the feeling rising from the pit of my stomach that something of great horror was about to unfold. Perhaps Uncle Philip was about to say something else – perhaps he had planned the whole thing quite differently – but at that moment, as we stood there jostled on all sides, I believe he saw in my face that the game was up. A terrible confusion passed across his features, then he said, barely audibly in the din:

"Good boy."

He grasped my shoulder, again and let his gaze wander about him. Then he appeared to come to a decision I had already anticipated.

"Good boy!" he said, this time more loudly, his voice trembling with emotion. Then he added: "I didn't want you hurt. You understand that? I didn't want you hurt."

With that he spun round and vanished into the crowd.

Kazuo Ishiguro

VANITY FAIR

Downstairs, then, they went, Joseph very red and blushing, Rebecca very modest, and holding her green eyes downwards. She was dressed in white, with bare shoulders as white as snow – the picture of youth, unprotected innocence, and humble virgin simplicity. "I must be very quiet," thought Rebecca, "and very much interested about India."

Now we have heard how Mrs Sedley had prepared a fine curry for her son, just as he liked it, and in the course of dinner a portion of this dish was offered to Rebecca. "What is it?" said she, turning an appealing look to Mr Joseph.

"Capital," said he. His mouth was full of it: his face quite red with the delightful exercise of gobbling. "Mother, it's as good as my own curries in India."

"Oh, I must try some, if it is an Indian dish," said Miss Rebecca. "I am sure everything must be good that comes from there."

"Give Miss Sharp some curry, my dear," said Mr Sedley, laughing.

Rebecca had never tasted the dish before.

"Do you find it as good as everything else from India?" said Mr Sedley.

"Oh, excellent!" said Rebecca, who was suffering tortures with the cayenne pepper.

"Try a chili with it, Miss Sharp," said Joseph, really interested.

"A chili," said Rebecca, gasping. "Oh yes!" She thought a chili was something cool, as its name imported, and was served with some. "How fresh and green they look," she said, and put one into her mouth. It was hotter than the curry; flesh and blood could bear it no longer. She laid down her fork. "Water, for Heaven's sake, water!" she cried. Mr Sedley burst out laughing (he was a coarse man, from the Stock Exchange, where they love all sorts of practical jokes). "They are real Indian, I assure you," said he. "Sambo, give Miss Sharp some water."

William Thackeray

THE TIME MACHINE

I fancied I heard the breathing of a crowd of those dreadful little beings about me. I felt the box of matches in my hand being gently disengaged, and other hands behind me plucking at my clothing. The sense of these unseen creatures examining me was indescribably unpleasant. The sudden realization of my ignorance of their ways of thinking and doing came home to me very vividly in the darkness. I shouted at them as loudly as I could. They started away, and then I could feel them approaching me again. They clutched at me more boldly, whispering odd sounds to each other. I shivered violently, and shouted again – rather discordantly. This time they were not so seriously alarmed, and they made a queer laughing noise as they came back at me. I will confess I was horribly frightened. I determined to strike another match and escape under the protection of its glare. I did so, and eking out the flicker with a scrap of paper from my pocket, I made good my retreat to the narrow tunnel. But I had scarce entered this when my light was blown out, and in the blackness I could hear the Morlocks rustling like wind among leaves, and pattering like the rain, as they hurried after me.

In a moment I was clutched by several hands, and there was no mistaking that they were trying to haul me back. I struck another light, and waved it in their dazzled faces. You can scarce imagine how nauseatingly inhuman they looked – those pale, chinless faces and great, lidless, pinkish-grey eyes! – as they stared in their blindness and bewilderment. But I did not stay to look, I promise you: I retreated again, and when my second match had ended, I struck my third. It had almost burned through when I reached the opening into the shaft. I lay down on the edge, for the throb of the great pump below made me giddy. Then I felt sideways for the projecting hooks, and, as I did so, my feet were grasped from behind, and I was violently tugged backward.

H G Wells

GRADE SEVEN –
SILVER MEDAL *SHAKESPEARE*

AS YOU LIKE IT
Act II, Scene VII

Blow, blow, thou winter wind,
Thou art not so unkind
        As man's ingratitude.
Thy tooth is not so keen,
Because thou art not seen,
        Although thy breath be rude.
Heigh-ho, sing heigh-ho, unto the green holly
Most friendship is feigning, most loving mere folly.
Then heigh-ho, the holly,
        This life is most jolly.

Freeze, freeze, thou bitter sky,
That dost not bite so nigh
        As benefits forgot.
Though thou the waters warp,
Thy sting is not so sharp,
        As friend remember'd not.
Heigh-ho, sing heigh-ho, unto the green holly,
Most friendship is feigning, most loving mere folly.
Then heigh-ho the holly,
This life is most jolly.

CYMBELINE
Act IV, Scene II

Fear no more the heat o' th' sun,
  Nor the furious winter's rages,
Thou thy worldly task has done,
  Home art gone and ta'en thy wages.
Golden lads and girls all must,
As chimney-sweepers, come to dust.

Fear no more the frown o' th' great,
  Thou art past the tyrant's stroke,
Care no more to clothe and eat,
  To thee the reed is as the oak:
The sceptre, learning, physic, must
All follow this and come to dust.

Fear no more the lightning-flash.
  Nor th' all-dreaded thunder-stone.
Fear not slander, censure rash.
  Thou hast finish'd joy and moan.
All lovers young, all lovers must
Consign to thee and come to dust.

No exorciser harm thee!
Nor no witchcraft charm thee!
Ghost unlaid forbear thee!
Nothing ill come near thee!
Quiet consummation have,
And renowned be thy grave!

ROMEO AND JULIET
Act II, Prologue

Chorus

Now old desire doth in his deathbed lie
And young affection gapes to be his heir;
That fair for which love groan'd for and would die,
With tender Juliet match'd, is now not fair.
Now Romeo is belov'd and loves again,
Alike bewitched by the charm of looks,
But to his foe suppos'd he must complain
And she steal love's sweet bait from fearful hooks.
Being held a foe, he may not have access
To breathe such vows as lovers use to swear;
And she as much in love, her means much less
To meet her new beloved anywhere.
But passion lends them power, time means, to meet,
Tempering extremities with extreme sweet.   (*Exit.*)

THE PASSIONATE PILGRIM, VIII

If music and sweet poetry agree,
As they must needs, the sister and the brother,
Then must the love be great 'twixt thee and me,
Because thou lov'st the one, and I the other.
Dowland to thee is dear, whose heavenly touch
Upon the lute doth ravish human sense;
Spenser to me, whose deep conceit is such
As, passing all conceit, needs no defence.
Thou lov'st to hear the sweet melodious sound
That Phoebus' lute, the queen of music, makes;
And I in deep delight am chiefly drown'd
Whenas himself to singing he betakes.
One god is god of both, as poets feign;
One knight loves both, and both in thee remain.

SONNET XXIX

When in disgrace with fortune and men's eyes
I all alone beweep my outcast state,
And trouble deaf heav'n with my bootless cries,
And look upon myself, and curse my fate,
Wishing me like to one more rich in hope,
Featured like him, like him with friends possessed,
Desiring this man's art and that man's scope,
With what I most enjoy contented least;
Yet in these thoughts myself almost despising,
Haply I think on thee, and then my state,
Like to the lark at break of day arising,
From sullen earth sings hymns at heaven's gate;
     For thy sweet love remembered such wealth brings
     That then I scorn to change my state with kings.

SONNET LX

Like as the waves make towards the pebbled shore,
So do our minutes hasten to their end,
Each changing place with that which goes before,
In sequent toil all forwards do contend.
Nativity, once in the main of light,
Crawls to maturity; wherewith being crowned
Crooked eclipses 'gainst his glory fight,
And time, that gave, doth now his gift confound.
Time doth transfix the flourish set on youth,
And delves the parallels in beauty's brow;
Feeds on the rarities of nature's truth,
And nothing stands but for his scythe to mow.
     And yet to times in hope my verse shall stand,
     Praising thy worth, despite his cruel hand.

SONNET LXI

Is it thy will thy image should keep open
My heavy eyelids to the weary night?
Dost thou desire my slumbers should be broken
While shadows like to thee do mock my sight?
Is it thy spirit that thou send'st from thee
So far from home into my deeds to pry,
To find out shames and idle hours in me,
The scope and tenor of thy jealousy?
O no, thy love, though much, is not so great;
It is my love that keeps mine eye awake,
Mine own true love that doth my rest defeat,
To play the watchman ever for thy sake.
      For thee watch I, whilst thou dost wake elsewhere,
      From me far off, with others all too near.

SONNET CXXX

My mistress' eyes are nothing like the sun;
Coral is far more red than her lips' red;
If snow be white, why then her breasts are dun;
If hairs be wires, black wires grow on her head;
I have seen roses damasked, red and white,
But no such roses see I in her cheeks;
And in some perfumes is there more delight
Than in the breath that from my mistress reeks.
I love to hear her speak, yet well I know
That music hath a far more pleasing sound;
I grant I never saw a goddess go;
My mistress when she walks treads on the ground.
      And yet, by heaven, I think my love as rare
      As any she belied with false compare.

GRADE EIGHT –
GOLD MEDAL *VERSE*

PENITENCE

I was driving into the wind
on a northern road,
the redwoods swaying around me like a black
ocean.
          I'd drifted off: I didn't see the deer
till it bounced away,
the back legs swinging outwards as I braked
and swerved into the tinder
of the verge.
              Soon as I stopped
the headlamps filled with moths
and something beyond the trees was tuning in,
a hard attention
boring through my flesh
to stroke the bone.
                That shudder took so long
to end, I thought the animal had slipped
beneath the wheels, and lay there
quivering.
          I left the engine running; stepped outside;
away, at the edge of the light, a body
shifted amongst the leaves
and I wanted to go, to help, to make it well,
but every step I took
pushed it away.
              Or – no; that's not the truth,
or all the truth:
now I admit my own fear held me back,
not fear of the dark, or that presence
bending the trees;
not even fear, exactly, but the dread
of touching, of colliding with that pain.

I stood there, in the river of the wind,
for minutes; then I walked back to the car
and drove away.
                    I want to think that deer
survived; or, if it died,
it slipped into the blackness unawares.
But now and then I drive out to the woods
and park the car: the headlamps fill with moths;
the woods tune in; I listen to the night
and hear an echo, fading through the trees,
my own flesh in the body of the deer
still resonant, remembered through the fender.

John Burnside

LA FIGLIA CHE PIANGE

O quam te memorem virgo –

Stand on the highest pavement of the stair –
Lean on a garden urn –
Weave, weave the sunlight in your hair –
Clasp your flowers to you with a pained surprise –
Fling them to the ground and turn
With a fugitive resentment in your eyes:
But weave, weave the sunlight in your hair.

So I would have had him leave,
So I would have had her stand and grieve,
So he would have left
As the soul leaves the body torn and bruised,
As the mind deserts the body it has used.
I should find
Some way incomparably light and deft,
Some way we both should understand,
Simple and faithless as a smile and shake of the hand.

She turned away, but with the autumn weather
Compelled my imagination many days,
Many days and many hours:
Her hair over her arms and her arms full of flowers.
And I wonder how they should have been together!
I should have lost a gesture and a pose.
Sometimes these cogitations still amaze
The troubled midnight and the noon's repose.

T S Eliot

CONSTANTLY RISKING ABSURDITY

Constantly risking absurdity
                    and death
    whenever he performs
                        above the heads
                            of his audience

the poet like an acrobat
                climbs on rime
                    to a high wire of his own making
and balancing on eyebeams
                        above a sea of faces
        paces his way
                    to the other side of day
performing entrechats
                    and sleight-of-foot tricks
and other high theatrics
                        and all without mistaking
        any thing
                for what it may not be

For he's the super realist
                who must perforce perceive
      taut truth
                before the taking of each stance or step
in his supposed advance
                    toward that still higher perch
where Beauty stands and waits
                with gravity
                      to start her death-defying leap

And he
      a little charleychaplin man
                    who may or may not catch
      her fair eternal form
                spreadeagled in the empty air
      of existence.

Lawrence Ferlinghetti

AT GRASS

The eye can hardly pick them out
From the cold shade they shelter in,
Till wind distresses tail and mane;
Then one crops grass, and moves about
– The other seeming to look on –
And stands anonymous again.

Yet fifteen years ago, perhaps
Two dozen distances sufficed
To fable them: faint afternoons
Of Cups and Stakes and Handicaps,
Whereby their names were artificed
To inlay faded, classic Junes –

Silks at the start: against the sky
Numbers and parasols: outside,
Squadrons of empty cars, and heat,
And littered grass: then the long cry
Hanging unhushed till it subside
To stop-press columns on the street.

Do memories plague their ears like flies?
They shake their heads. Dusk brims the shadows.
Summer by summer all stole away,
The starting-gates, the crowds and cries –
All but the unmolesting meadows.
Almanacked, their names live; they

Have slipped their names, and stand at ease,
Or gallop for what must be joy,
And not a fieldglass sees them home,
Or curious stop-watch prophesies:
Only the groom, and the groom's boy,
With bridles in the evening come.

Philip Larkin

SONNET

What lips my lips have kissed, and where, and why,
I have forgotten, and what arms have lain
Under my head till morning; but the rain
Is full of ghosts tonight, that tap and sigh
Upon the glass and listen for reply,
And in my heart there stirs a quiet pain
For unremembered lads that not again
Will turn to me at midnight with a cry.

Thus in the winter stands the lonely tree,
Nor knows what birds have vanished one by one,
Yet knows its boughs more silent than before:
I cannot say what loves have come and gone,
I only know that summer sang in me
A little while, that in me sings no more.

Edna St Vincent Millay

SOME BEASTS

It was early twilight of the iguana.

From his rainbow-crested ridging
his tongue sank like a dart
into the mulch,
the monastic ant-heap was melodiously
teeming in the undergrowth,
the guanaco, rarefied as oxygen
up among the cloud-plains,
wore gold-flecked boots,
while the llama opened candid
wide eyes in the delicacy
of a world filled with dew.
The monkeys wove a thread
interminably erotic
along the banks of dawn,
demolishing walls of pollen
and flushing the violet flight
of the butterflies from Buga.
It was night of the alligators,
pure and pullulating night
of snouts above the ooze
and from over the sleep-drenched bogs
a dull sound of armour
fell back upon the original earth.

The jaguar touches the leaves
with his phosphorescent absence,
the puma runs on the foliage
like all-consuming flame
and in him burn
the alcoholic eyes of the jungle.
The badgers scratch the river's
feet, scenting out the nest
whose throbbing delight
they'll assail red-toothed.

And in the deeps of great water
the giant anaconda lies
like the circle of the earth,
covered in ritual mud,
devouring and religious.

Pablo Neruda

IN THE ORCHARD

'I thought you loved me.' 'No, it was only fun.'
'When we stood there, closer than all?' 'Well, the harvest moon
Was shining and queer in your hair, and it turned my head.'
'That made you?' 'Yes.' 'Just the moon and the light it made
Under the tree?' 'Well, your mouth, too.' 'Yes, my mouth?'
'And the quiet there that sang like the drum in the booth.
You shouldn't have danced like that.' 'Like what?' 'So close,
With your head turned up, and the flower in your hair, a rose
That smelt all warm.' 'I loved you. I thought you knew
I wouldn't have danced like that with any but you.'
'I didn't know. I thought you knew it was fun.'
'I thought it was love you meant.' 'Well, it's done.' 'Yes, it's done.
I've seen boys stone a blackbird, and watched them drown
A kitten...it clawed at the reeds, and they pushed it down

Into the pool while it screamed. Is that fun, too?'
'Well, boys are like that... Your brothers...' 'Yes, I know.
But you, so lovely and strong! Not you! Not you!'
'They don't understand it's cruel. It's only a game.'
'And are girls fun, too?' 'No, still in a way it's the same.
It's queer and lovely to have a girl...' 'Go on.'
'It makes you mad for a bit to feel she's your own,
And you laugh and kiss her, and maybe you give her a ring,
But it's only in fun.' 'But I gave you everything.'
'Well, you shouldn't have done it. You know what a fellow thinks
When a girl does that.' 'Yes, he talks of her over his drinks
And calls her a—' 'Stop that now. I thought you knew.'
'But it wasn't with anyone else. It was only you.'
'How did I know? I thought you wanted it too.
I thought you were like the rest. Well, what's to be done?'
'To be done?' 'Is it all right?' 'Yes.' 'Sure?' 'Yes, but why?'
'I don't know. I thought you were going to cry.
You said you had something to tell me.' 'Yes, I know.
It wasn't anything really...I think I'll go.'
'Yes, it's late. There's thunder about, a drop of rain
Fell on my hand in the dark. I'll see you again
At the dance next week. You're sure that everything's right?'
'Yes.' 'Well, I'll be going.' 'Kiss me...' 'Good night.'... 'Good night.'

Muriel Stuart

A SATIRICAL ELEGY ON THE DEATH
OF A LATE FAMOUS GENERAL

His Grace! impossible! what dead!
Of old age too, and in his bed!
And could that Mighty Warrior fall?
And so inglorious, after all!
Well, since he's gone, no matter how,
The last loud trump must wake him now:
And, trust me, as the noise grows stronger,
He'd wish to sleep a little longer.
And could he be indeed so old
As by the news-papers we're told?
Threescore, I think, is pretty high;
'Twas time in conscience he should die.
This world he cumber'd long enough;
He burnt his candle to the snuff;
And that's the reason, some folks think,
He left behind *so great a stink.*
Behold his funeral appears,
Nor widow's sighs, nor orphan's tears,
Wont at such times each heart to pierce,
Attend the progress of his hearse.
But what of that, his friends may say,
He had those honours in his day.
True to his profit and his pride,
He made them weep before he dy'd.
    Come hither, all ye empty things,
Ye bubbles rais'd by breath of Kings;
Who float upon the tide of state,
Come hither, and behold your fate.
Let pride be taught by this rebuke,
How very mean a thing's a Duke;
From all his ill-got honours flung,
Turn'd to that dirt from whence he sprung.

Jonathan Swift

GRADE EIGHT –
GOLD MEDAL *PROSE*

EVA LUNA

The day the postman found Lukas Carlé's body, the forest was freshly washed, dripping and shining, and from its floor rose a strong breath of rotted leaves and a pale mist of another planet. For some forty years, every morning, the man had ridden his bicycle down the same path. Peddling that trail, he had earned his daily bread and had survived unharmed two wars, the occupation, hunger, and many other misfortunes. Because of his work, he knew all the inhabitants of the area by name and surname, just as he could identify every tree in the forest by its species and age. At first sight, that morning seemed no different from any other, the same oaks, beeches, chestnuts, birches, the same feathery moss and mushrooms at the base of the tallest trees, the same cool, fragrant breeze, the same shadows and patches of light. It was a day like all the rest, and perhaps a person with less knowledge of nature would not have noted the warnings, but the mailman was on edge, his skin prickling, because he perceived signs no other human eye would have registered. He always imagined the forest as a huge green beast with gentle blood flowing through its veins, a calm-spirited animal; but today it was restless. He got off his bicycle and sniffed the early morning air, seeking the reason for his uneasiness. The silence was so absolute he feared he had gone deaf. He laid his bicycle on the ground and took a couple of steps off the path to look around. He did not have to go far; there it was, waiting for him, hanging from a branch above his head, a thick cord around its neck. He did not need to see the hanged man's face to know who it was. He had known Lukas Carlé ever since he had arrived in the village years before – come from God knows where, somewhere in France, maybe, with his trunkloads of books, his map of the world, and his diploma – and immediately married the prettiest of the village girls, and within a few months destroyed her beauty. The mailman recognized Carlé by his high-top shoes and schoolmaster's smock, and he had the impression of having seen this scene before, as if for years he had been expecting a similar dénouement. At first he felt no panic, only a sense of irony, the urge to say to him: I warned you, you scoundrel. It was several seconds before he grasped the enormity of what had happened, and at that instant the tree groaned, the body slowly turned, and the hopeless eyes of the hanged man met his.

Isabel Allende

TRUE HISTORY OF THE KELLY GANG

Colonel Rede, the Sheriff for the Central Bailiwick, was attended by Mr Ellis, the Under-Sheriff, and presented himself at the door of the condemned cell punctually at 10 o'clock to demand the body of Edward Kelly in order to carry out the awful sentence of death. Mr Castieau, the Governor of Melbourne Gaol, had some little time previously visited the prisoner, and seen his irons knocked off; and the necessary warrant being presented by the Sheriff, he tapped at the door, and the prisoner was made acquainted with the fearful fact that his last hour had arrived. All this time Upjohn, the hangman, who was officiating in this horrible capacity for the first time, had remained unseen; but upon the door of Kelly's cell being opened, the signal was given and he emerged from the condemned cell opposite, now occupied by his first victim. He stepped across the scaffold quietly and, as he did so, quietly turned his head and looked down upon the spectators, revealing a fearfully repulsive countenance.

The hangman is an old man about 70 years of age, but broad-shouldered and burly. As he was serving a sentence when he volunteered for this dreadful office, and as that sentence is still unexpired, he is closely shaved and cropped, and wears the prison dress. Thick bristles of a pure white stick up all over his crown and provide him a ghastly appearance. He has heavy features altogether, the nose perhaps being the most striking and ugly.

As this was Upjohn's first attempt at hanging, Dr Barker was present alongside the drop, to see that the knot was placed in the right position. Upjohn disappeared into the condemned cell, and proceeded to pinion Kelly with a strong broad leather belt. The prisoner, however, remarked, "You need not pinion me," but was, of course, told that it was indispensable.

Preceded by the crucifix, which was held up before him by the officiating priests, Kelly was then led onto the platform. He had not been shaved or cropped, but was in prison clothes. He seemed calm and collected, but paler than usual, although this effect might have been produced by the white cap placed over his head, but not yet drawn down over his face. As he stepped on the drop, he remarked in a low tone, "Such is life."

Peter Carey

MIDDLEMARCH

"Is any one else coming to dine besides Mr Casaubon?"

"Not that I know of."

"I hope there is some one else. Then I shall not hear him eat his soup so."

"What is there remarkable about his soup-eating?"

"Really, Dodo, can't you hear how he scrapes his spoon? And he always blinks before he speaks. I don't know whether Locke blinked, but I'm sure I am sorry for those who sat opposite to him, if he did."

"Celia," said Dorothea, with emphatic gravity, "pray don't make any more observations of that kind."

"Why not? They are quite true," returned Celia, who had her reasons for persevering, though she was beginning to be a little afraid.

"Many things are true which only the commonest minds observe."

"Then I think the commonest minds must be rather useful. I think it is a pity Mr Casaubon's mother had not a commoner mind: she might have taught him better." Celia was inwardly frightened, and ready to run away, now she had hurled this light javelin.

Dorothea's feelings had gathered to an avalanche, and there could be no further preparation.

"It is right to tell you, Celia, that I am engaged to marry Mr Casaubon."

Perhaps Celia had never turned so pale before. The paper man she was making would have had his leg injured, but for her habitual care of whatever she held in her hands. She laid the fragile figure down at once, and sat perfectly still for a few moments. When she spoke there was a tear gathering.

"Oh, Dodo, I hope you will be happy." Her sisterly tenderness could not but surmount other feelings at this moment, and her fears were the fears of affection.

Dorothea was still hurt and agitated.

"It is quite decided, then?" said Celia, in an awed undertone. "And uncle knows?"

"I have accepted Mr Casaubon's offer. My uncle brought me the letter that contained it; he knew about it beforehand."

"I beg your pardon, if I have said anything to hurt you, Dodo," said Celia, with a slight sob. She never could have thought that she should feel as she did. There was something funereal in the whole affair, and Mr Casaubon seemed to be the officiating clergyman, about whom it would be indecent to make remarks.

George Eliot

WASHINGTON SQUARE

He let her alone for six months more—six months during which she accommodated herself without a protest to the extension of their tour. But he spoke again at the end of this time: It was at the very last, the night before they embarked for New York, in the hotel at Liverpool. They had been dining together in a great, dim, musty sitting room; and then the cloth had been removed, and the doctor walked slowly up and down. Catherine at last took her candle to go to bed, but her father motioned her to stay.

"What do you mean to do when you get home?" he asked, while she stood there with her candle in her hand.

"Do you mean about Mr Townsend?"

"About Mr Townsend."

"We shall probably marry."

The doctor took several turns again while she waited. "Do you hear from him as much as ever?"

"Yes, twice a month," said Catherine, promptly.

"And does he always talk about marriage?"

"Oh yes; that is, he talks about other things too, but he always says something about that."

"I am glad to hear he varies his subjects; his letters might otherwise be monotonous."

"He writes beautifully," said Catherine, who was very glad of a chance to say it.

"They always write beautifully. However, in a given case that doesn't diminish the merit. So, as soon as you arrive, you are going off with him?"

This seemed a rather gross way of putting it, and something that there was of dignity in Catherine resented it. "I cannot tell you till we arrive," she said.

"That's reasonable enough," her father answered. "That's all I ask of you—that you *do* tell me, that you give me definite notice. When a poor man is to lose his only child, he likes to have an inkling of it beforehand."

"Oh, Father, you will not lose me," Catherine said, spilling her candle-wax.

"Three days before will do," he went on, "if you are in a position to be positive then. He ought to be very thankful to me, do you know. I have done a mighty good thing for him in taking you abroad; your value is twice as great, with all the knowledge and taste that you have acquired. A year ago, you were perhaps a little limited—a little rustic; but now you have seen everything, and appreciated everything, and you will be a most entertaining companion. We have fattened the sheep for him before he kills it." Catherine turned away, and stood staring at the blank door. "Go to bed," said her father, "and as we don't go aboard till noon, you may sleep late. We shall probably have a most uncomfortable voyage."

Henry James

GRACE NOTES

Immediately she was aware of its femininity, this tiny wizened red girl. She was very fine, her hair Brylcreemed and flat and wet to her head. The wings of her tiny nostrils flared as she tried to breathe, her eyelids clenched against the harsh lights of the theatre. Its pores were clean white pin-points. The mother probed into the blanket and took out a fist to check for herself. The fingers tiny, ending in the most perfect crescent nails. She put the baby to her face and touched their cheeks together. It opened its mouth and gave a gummy yawn. Catherine realised that she was crying and heard herself saying – she's lovely, she's lovely, she's lovely. A vow welled up in her that this creature she had given birth to must never, never come to any harm. She must be protected with all her strength and love and care. She must surround and envelop her. She kissed her and the baby's eyes opened fractionally to reveal grape-purple pupils at east and west and the mother laughed, still crying.

As the nurse took the baby away for tests Catherine saw the perfection of her daughter's ear, whorled and tiny and precise as a shore shell. There was so much of her they hadn't allowed her to see.

They cleaned Catherine up and wheeled her back to a different ward and gave her a cup of tea and toast. The tea was hot and strong. She felt she could fly – she felt light with love. For her girl, for herself. For all the other women in the world who had ever given birth. Especially for her own mother – the feeling was totally unexpected, came from nowhere into her. She wanted to be with her mother, they had both shared an experience which should unite them in love. She wanted to tell her as another mother, as an equal about her girl child who would some day, maybe, give birth to her own girl.

Bernard MacLaverty

A FINE BALANCE

"If your hair business collapsed, wouldn't it have been easier to collect something else? Newspapers, dabba, bottles?"

"I have been asking myself the same question. The answer is yes. There were dozens of possibilities. At the very worst, I could have become a beggar. Even that would have been preferable to the horrible road I was starting on. It's easy to see now. But a blindness had come over me. The more difficult it was to collect long hair, the more desperately I wanted to succeed, as though my life depended on it. And so my scheme did not seem at all crazy."

In fact, when it was put to work, he realized he had developed a brilliant system. With his cloth bag and scissors he would elbow himself into a crowd, selecting the victim (or beneficiary) with care, never impatient and never greedy. A head with two plaits could not tempt him to go for both – he was happy with one. And he always resisted the urge to cut too close to the nape – the extra inch or two could be his undoing.

In the bazaar, Rajaram stayed clear of the shoppers who came with servants, no matter how luxuriant the hair. Similarly, matrons with children in tow were avoided – youngsters were unpredictable. The women he singled out to receive the grace of his scissors would be alone, preferably someone poorly dressed, engrossed in buying vegetables for her family, agitated by the high prices, bargaining tenaciously, or absorbed in watching the vendor's weights and scales to make sure she wasn't short-changed.

Soon, though, she would be short-haired. Amid the milling shoppers, Rajaram's sharp instrument emerged unnoticed. It went snip, once, quickly and cleanly. The plait dropped into the cloth bag, and he disappeared, having delivered one more fellow human of the hindrance that, unbeknown to her, was weighing her down.

At bus stops, Rajaram chose the woman most anxious about her purse, clamped tight under her arm, its leather or plastic hot against her sweltering skin. Semicircles of sweat would be travelling like an epidemic across her blouse. He would join the commuters, another weary worker returning home. And when the bus's arrival converted the queue into a charging horde, the nervous woman hesitated at the periphery long enough for the scissors to do their work.

He never operated twice in the same marketplace or at the same bus stop. That would be too risky.

Rohinton Mistry

HERE WE ARE
(a short story from *Complete Stories*)

"Is there anything special you want to do tonight?"

"What?" she said.

"What I mean to say," he said, "would you like to go to a show or something?"

"Why, whatever you like," she said. "I sort of didn't think people went to theaters and things on their—I mean, I've got a couple of letters I simply must write. Don't let me forget."

"Oh," he said. "You're going to write letters tonight?"

"Well, you see," she said. "I've been perfectly terrible. What with all the excitement and everything. I never did thank poor old Mrs. Sprague for her berry spoon, and I never did a thing about those book ends the McMasters sent. It's just too awful of me. I've got to write them this very night."

"And when you've finished writing your letters," he said, "maybe I could get you a magazine or a bag of peanuts."

"What?" she said.

"I mean," he said, "I wouldn't want you to be bored."

"As if I could be bored with you!" she said. "Silly! Aren't we married? Bored!"

"What I thought," he said, "I thought when we got in, we could go right up to the Biltmore and anyway leave our bags, and maybe have a little dinner in the room, kind of quiet, and then do whatever we wanted. I mean. I mean—well, let's go right up there from the station."

"Oh, yes, let's," she said. "I'm so glad we're going to the Biltmore. I just love it. The twice I've stayed in New York we've always stayed there, Papa and Mamma and Ellie and I, and I was crazy about it. I always sleep so well there. I go right off to sleep the minute I put my head on the pillow."

"Oh, you do?" he said.

"At least, I mean," she said. "Way up high it's so quiet."

"We might go to some show or other tomorrow night instead of tonight," he said. "Don't you think that would be better?"

"Yes, I think it might," she said.

He rose, balanced a moment, crossed over and sat down beside her.

"Do you really have to write those letters tonight?" he said.

"Well," she said, "I don't suppose they'd get there any quicker than if I wrote them tomorrow."

There was a silence with things going on in it.

Dorothy Parker

DRACULA

Outside the Harkers' door we paused. Art and Quincey held back, and the latter said:-

"Should we disturb her?"

"We must," said Van Helsing grimly. "If the door be locked, I shall break it in."

"May it not frighten her terribly? It is unusual to break into a lady's room!" Van Helsing said solemnly –

"You are always right; but this is life and death. All chambers are alike to the doctor; and even were they not they are all as one to me tonight. Friend John, when I turn the handle, if the door does not open, do you put your shoulder down and shove; and you too, my friends. Now!"

He turned the handle as he spoke, but the door did not yield. We threw ourselves against it; with a crash it burst open, and we almost fell headlong into the room. The Professor did actually fall, and I saw across him as he gathered himself up from hands and knees. What I saw appalled me. I felt my hair rise like bristles on the back of my neck, and my heart seemed to stand still.

The moonlight was so bright that through the thick yellow blind the room was light enough to see. On the bed beside the window lay Jonathan Harker, his face flushed and breathing heavily as though in a stupor. Kneeling on the near edge of the bed facing outwards was the white-clad figure of his wife. By her side stood a tall, thin man, clad in black. His face was turned from us, but the instant we saw we all recognized the Count – in every way, even to the scar on his forehead. With his left hand he held both Mrs Harker's hands, keeping them away with her arms at full tension; his right hand gripped her by the back of the neck, forcing her face down on his bosom. Her white nightdress was smeared with blood, and a thin stream trickled down the man's bare breast which was shown by his torn-open dress. The attitude of the two had a terrible resemblance to a child forcing a kitten's nose into a saucer of milk to compel it to drink. As we burst into the room, the Count turned his face, and the hellish look that I had heard described seemed to leap into it. His eyes flamed red with devilish passion; the great nostrils of the white aquiline nose opened wide and quivered at the edge; and the white sharp teeth, behind the full lips of the blood-dripping mouth, clamped together like those of a wild beast. With a wrench, which threw his victim back upon the bed as though hurled from a height, he turned and sprang at us. But by this time the Professor had gained his feet, and was holding towards him the envelope which contained the Sacred Wafer. The Count suddenly stopped, just as poor Lucy had done outside the tomb, and cowered back. Further and further back he cowered, as we, lifting our crucifixes, advanced. The moonlight suddenly failed, as a great black cloud sailed across the sky; and when the gaslight sprang up under Quincey's match, we saw nothing but a faint vapour.

Bram Stoker

GRADE EIGHT –
GOLD MEDAL *SHAKESPEARE*

ANTONY AND CLEOPATRA
Act II, Scene II

Enobarbus
    The barge she sat in, like a burnished throne,
    Burned on the water; the poop was beaten gold;
    Purple the sails, and so perfumed that
    The winds were love-sick with them; the oars were silver,
    Which to the tune of flutes kept stroke, and made
    The water which they beat to follow faster,
    As amorous of their strokes. For her own person,
    It beggared all description: she did lie
    In her pavilion, cloth-of-gold of tissue,
    O'erpicturing that Venus where we see
    The fancy outwork nature. On each side her
    Stood pretty dimpled boys, like smiling cupids,
    With divers-coloured fans, whose wind did seem
    To glow the delicate cheeks which they did cool,
    And what they undid did.
    …

    Her gentlewoman, like the Nereides,
    So many mermaids, tended her i'th' eyes,
    And made their bends adornings. At the helm
    A seeming mermaid steers. The silken tackle
    Swell with the touches of those flower-soft hands
    That yarely frame the office. From the barge
    A strange invisible perfume hits the sense
    Of the adjacent wharfs. The city cast
    Her people out upon her, and Antony,
    Enthroned i'th' market-place, did sit alone,
    Whistling to th'air, which, but for vacancy,
    Had gone to gaze on Cleopatra, too,
    And made a gap in nature.
    …

Age cannot wither her, nor custom stale
Her infinite variety. Other women cloy
The appetites they feed, but she makes hungry
Where most she satisfies; for vilest things
Become themselves in her, that the holy priests
Bless her when she is riggish.

AS YOU LIKE IT
Act II, Scene VII

Jaques

All the world's a stage,
And all the men and women merely players.
They have their exits and their entrances,
And one man in his time plays many parts,
His acts being seven ages. At first the infant,
Mewling and puking in the nurse's arms.
Then, the whining school-boy with his satchel
And shining morning face, creeping like a snail
Unwillingly to school. And then the lover,
Sighing like furnace, with woeful ballad
Made to his mistress' eyebrow. Then, a soldier,
Full of strange oaths, and bearded like the pard,
Jealous in honour, sudden, and quick in quarrel,
Seeking the bubble reputation
Even in the cannon's mouth. And then, the justice,
In fair round belly, with good capon lin'd,
With eyes severe, and beard of formal cut,
Full of wise saws, and modern instances,
And so he plays his part. The sixth age shifts
Into the lean and slipper'd pantaloon,
With spectacles on nose, and pouch on side,
His youthful hose well sav'd, a world too wide

For his shrunk shank, and his big manly voice,
Turning again toward childish treble, pipes
And whistles in his sound. Last scene of all,
That ends this strange eventful history,
Is second childishness and mere oblivion,
Sans teeth, sans eyes, sans taste, sans everything.

KING HENRY IV
Part Two: Induction

Rumour

Open your ears; for which of you will stop
The vent of hearing when loud Rumour speaks?
I, from the Orient to the drooping West,
Making the wind my post-horse, still unfold
The acts commenced on this ball of earth.
Upon my tongues continual slanders ride,
The which in every language I pronounce,
Stuffing the ears of men with false reports.
I speak of peace, while covert enmity
Under the smile of safety wounds the world;
And who but Rumour, who but only I,
Make fearful musters, and prepar'd defence,
Whiles the big year, swoln with some other grief,
Is thought with child by the stern tyrant War,
And no such matter? Rumour is a pipe
Blown by surmises, jealousies, conjectures,
And of so easy and so plain a stop
That the blunt monster with uncounted heads,
The still-discordant wav'ring multitude,
Can play upon it. But what need I thus
My well-known body to anatomize
Among my household? Why is Rumour here?

I run before King Harry's victory,
Who in a bloody field by Shrewsbury
Hath beaten down young Hotspur and his troops,
Quenching the flame of bold rebellion
Even with the rebel's blood. But what mean I
To speak so true at first? My office is
To noise abroad that Harry Monmouth fell
Under the wrath of noble Hotspur's sword,
And that the King before the Douglas' rage
Stoop'd his anointed head as low as death.
This have I rumour'd through the peasant towns
Between that royal field of Shrewsbury
And this worm-eaten hold of ragged stone,
Where Hotspur's father, old Northumberland,
Lies crafty-sick. The posts come tiring on,
And not a man of them brings other news
Than they have learnt of me. From Rumour's tongues
They bring smooth comforts false, worse than true wrongs.

KING HENRY V
Prologue

Chorus
O for a muse of fire, that would ascend
The brightest heaven of invention,
A kingdom for a stage, princes to act,
And monarchs to behold the swelling scene!
Then should the warlike Harry, like himself,
Assume the port of Mars, and at his heels,
Leashed in like hounds, should famine, sword and fire
Crouch for employment. But pardon, gentles all,
The flat unraised spirits that hath dared
On this unworthy scaffold to bring forth

So great an object. Can this cockpit hold
The vasty fields of France? Or may we cram
Within this wooden O the very casques
That did affright the air at Agincourt?
O pardon, since a crooked figure may
Attest in little place a million,
And let us, ciphers to this great account,
On your imaginary forces work.
Suppose within the girdle of these walls
Are now confined two mighty monarchies,
Whose high upreared and abutting fronts
The perilous narrow ocean parts asunder.
Piece out our imperfections with your thoughts.
Into a thousand parts divide one man
And make imaginary puissance.
Think, when we talk of horses, that you see them
Printing their proud hoofs i' th' receiving earth.
For 'tis your thoughts that now must deck our kings,
Carry them here and there, jumping o'er times,
Turning th' accomplishment of many years
Into an hour-glass: for the which supply,
Admit me Chorus to this history,
Who prologue-like your humble patience pray,
Gently to hear, kindly to judge our play.

KING HENRY V
Act IV

Chorus

Now entertain conjecture of time
When creeping murmur and the poring dark
Fills the wide vessel of the universe.
From camp to camp through the foul womb of night

The hum of either army stilly sounds,
That the fixed sentinels almost receive
The secret whispers of each other's watch.
Fire answers fire, and through their paly flames
Each battle sees the other's umbered face.
Steed threatens steed, in high and boastful neighs
Piercing the night's dull ear; and from the tents
The armourers accomplishing the knights,
With busy hammers closing rivets up,
Give dreadful note of preparation.
The country cocks do crow, the clocks do toll,
And the third hour of drowsy morning name.
Proud of their numbers and secure in soul,
The confident and over-lusty French
Do the low-rated English play at dice,
And chide the cripple tardy-gaited night
Who like a foul and ugly witch doth limp
So tediously away. The poor condemned English,
Like sacrifices, by their watchful fires
Sit patiently and inly ruminate
The morning's danger; and their gesture sad,
Investing lank-lean cheeks and war-worn coats,
Presenteth them unto the gazing moon
So many horrid ghosts. O now, who will behold
The royal captain of his ruined band
Walking from watch to watch, from tent to tent,
Let him cry 'Praise and glory on his head!'
For forth he goes and visits all his host,
Bids them good morrow with a modest smile,
And calls them brothers, friends and countrymen.
Upon his royal face there is no note
How dread an army hath enrounded him,
Nor doth he dedicate one jot of colour

Unto the weary and all-watched night,
But freshly looks and overbears attaint
With cheerful semblance and sweet majesty,
That every wretch, pining and pale before,
Beholding him plucks comfort from his looks.

ROMEO AND JULIET
Act I, Scene IV

Mercutio

O then I see Queen Mab hath been with you.
She is the fairies' midwife, and she comes
In shape no bigger than an agate stone
On the forefinger of an alderman,
Drawn with a team of little atomi
Over men's noses as they lie asleep.
Her chariot is an empty hazelnut
Made by the joiner squirrel or old grub,
Time out o' mind the fairies' coachmakers;
Her wagon-spokes made of long spinners' legs,
The cover of the wings of grasshoppers,
Her traces of the smallest spider web,
Her collars of the moonshine's watery beams,
Her whip of cricket's bone, the lash of film,
Her waggoner, a small grey-coated gnat,
Not half so big as a round little worm
Prick'd from the lazy finger of a maid;
And in this state she gallops night by night
Through lovers' brains, and then they dream of love;
O'er courtiers' knees, that dream on curtsies straight;
O'er lawyers' fingers who straight dream on fees;
O'er ladies' lips, who straight on kisses dream,
Which oft the angry Mab with blisters plagues

Because their breaths with sweetmeats tainted are.
Sometime she gallops o'er a courtier's nose
And then dreams he of smelling out a suit;
And sometime comes she with a tithe-pig's tail,
Tickling a parson's nose as a lies asleep;
Then dreams he of another benefice.
Sometime she driveth o'er a soldier's neck
And then dreams he of cutting foreign throats,
Of breaches, ambuscados, Spanish blades,
Of healths five fathom deep; and then anon
Drums in his ear, at which he starts and wakes,
And being thus frighted swears a prayer or two
And sleeps again. This is that very Mab
That plaits the manes of horses in the night
And bakes the elf-locks in foul sluttish hairs,
Which, once untangled, much misfortune bodes.
This is the hag, when maids lie on their backs,
That presses them and learns them first to bear,
Making them women of good carriage.
This is she—

THE WINTER'S TALE
Act IV, Scene I

Time

I that please some, try all: both joy and terror
Of good and bad, that makes and unfolds error,
Now take upon me, in the name of Time,
To use my wings. Impute it not a crime
To me, or my swift passage, that I slide
O'er sixteen years, and leave the growth untried
Of that wide gap, since it is in my power
To o'erthrow law, and in one self-born hour

To plant and o'erwhelm custom. Let me pass
The same I am, ere ancient'st order was,
Or what is now receiv'd. I witness to
The times that brought them in; so shall I do
To th' freshest things now reigning, and make stale
The glistering of this present, as my tale
Now seems to it. Your patience this allowing,
I turn my glass, and give my scene such growing
As you had slept between: Leontes leaving,
Th' effects of his fond jealousies so grieving
That he shuts up himself, imagine me,
Gentle spectators, that I now may be
In fair Bohemia, and remember well
I mentioned a son o' th' king's, which Florizel
I now name to you; and with speed so pace
To speak of Perdita, now grown in grace
Equal with wond'ring. What of her ensues
I list not prophesy; but let Time's news
Be known when 'tis brought forth. A shepherd's daughter,
And what to her adheres, which follows after,
Is th' argument of Time. Of this allow,
If ever you have spent time worse ere now;
If never, yet that Time himself doth say,
He wishes earnestly you never may.

TROILUS AND CRESSIDA
Prologue

Prologue

In Troy, there lies the scene. From Isles of Greece
The princes orgulous, their high blood chaf'd,
Have to the port of Athens sent their ships
Fraught with the ministers and instruments

Of cruel war: sixty and nine that wore
Their crownets regal, from th' Athenian bay
Put forth toward Phrygia, and their vow is made
To ransack Troy, within whose strong immures
The ravish'd Helen, Menelaus' queen,
With wanton Paris sleeps—and that's the quarrel.
To Tenedos they come,
And the deep-drawing barks do there disgorge
Their warlike fraughtage. Now on Dardan plains
The fresh and yet unbruised Greeks do pitch
Their brave pavilions: Priam's six-gated city,
Dardan and Timbria, Helias, Chetas, Troien,
And Antenorides, with massy staples
And co-responsive and fulfilling bolts,
Stir up the sons of Troy.
Now expectation, tickling skittish spirits
On one and other side, Trojan and Greek,
Sets all on hazard. And hither am I come,
A Prologue arm'd, but not in confidence
Of author's pen or actor's voice, but suited
In like conditions as our argument,
To tell you, fair beholders, that our play
Leaps o'er the vaunt and firstlings of those broils,
Beginning in the middle, starting thence away
To what may be digested in a play.
Like, or find fault: do as your pleasures are:
Now good, or bad, 'tis but the chance of war.

Publication Details for Prose Selections

GRADE TWO

The Little Mermaid (from *The Complete Fairy Tales and Stories*) by Hans
Christian Andersen, Anchor Books/Doubleday (ISBN: 0385189516).
Candidates must perform the extract as printed in this Anthology;
however, when reading the complete story in preparation for the
examination, other translations may be used.

The Peppermint Pig by Nina Bawden, Puffin Books (ISBN: 0140309446)

The Angel of Nitshill Road by Anne Fine, Egmont Books
(ISBN: 1405201843)

The Voyage of the Dawn Treader by C S Lewis, Collins
(ISBN: 0006716806)

The Great Piratical Rumbustification by Margaret Mahy, Puffin Books
(ISBN: 0140312617)

A Dog So Small by Philippa Pearce, Puffin Books (ISBN: 0140302069)

A Walk in Wolf Wood by Mary Stewart, Hodder Children's Books
(ISBN: 0340796634)

Juliet's Story by William Trevor, Red Fox (ISBN: 0099417731)

GRADE THREE

The Cuckoo Sister by Vivien Alcock, Heinemann Educational
(ISBN: 0435123270)

Skellig by David Almond, Hodder Children's Books (ISBN: 0340716002)

King of Shadows by Susan Cooper, Puffin Books (ISBN: 0141307994)

William Again by Richmal Crompton, Macmillan Children's Books
(ISBN: 033366227X)

Stormbreaker by Anthony Horowitz, Walker Books (ISBN: 074455943X)

The Phantom Tollbooth by Norton Juster, Collins (ISBN: 0006754252)

The Amber Spyglass by Philip Pullman, Scholastic (ISBN: 043999358X)

Holes by Louis Sachar, Bloomsbury (ISBN: 074754459X)

GRADE FOUR

Arthur: at the Crossing-places by Kevin Crossley-Holland, Orion
    Children's Books (ISBN: 1842552007)
Coram Boy by Jamila Gavin, Mammoth (ISBN: 0749732687)
The Nature of the Beast by Janni Howker, Walker Books
    (ISBN: 0744590329)
Journey to the River Sea by Eva Ibbotson, Macmillan Children's Books
    (ISBN: 033039715X)
Tug of War by Joan Lingard, Puffin Books (ISBN: 0140373195)
The Wind Singer by William Nicholson, Mammoth (ISBN: 0749744715)
The Rinaldi Ring by Jenny Nimmo, Mammoth (ISBN: 0749728191)
Face by Benjamin Zephaniah, Bloomsbury Children's Books
    (ISBN: 074754154X)

GRADE FIVE

The Hitchhiker's Guide to the Galaxy by Douglas Adams, Pan Macmillan
    (ISBN: 0330258648)
How It Happened (from *Tales of Unease*) by Sir Arthur Conan Doyle,
    Wordsworth Editions Ltd. (ISBN: 1840224061)
Roses from the Earth: The Biography of Anne Frank by Carol Ann Lee,
    Penguin Books (ISBN: 0140276289)
Three Men in a Boat by Jerome K Jerome, Penguin Books
    (ISBN: 0140621334)
The Lady and the Squire by Terry Jones, Puffin Books
    (ISBN: 0141307374)
The Gift of the Magi (from *100 Selected Stories*) by O Henry, Wordsworth
    Editions Ltd. (ISBN: 1853262412)
Wyrd Sisters by Terry Pratchett, Corgi Adult (ISBN: 0552134600)
Around the World in Eighty Days by Jules Verne, Wordsworth Editions Ltd.
    (ISBN: 1853260908)

GRADE SIX – BRONZE MEDAL

Pride and Prejudice by Jane Austen, Penguin Books (ISBN: 0140620222)
Hard Times by Charles Dickens, Penguin Books (ISBN: 0140620443)
Rebecca by Daphne du Maurier, Virago Press (ISBN: 1844080382)
Chocolat by Joanne Harris, Bantam (ISBN: 0552998486)
The Strange Case of Dr Jekyll and Mr Hyde by Robert Louis Stevenson,
    Canongate Classics (ISBN: 1841951560)
The Fellowship of the Ring by J R R Tolkien, HarperCollins
    (ISBN: 0007149212)
The Nightingale and the Rose (from *The Happy Prince and Other Stories*)
    by Oscar Wilde, Puffin Books (ISBN: 0140366911)
Flush by Virginia Woolf, Oxford Paperpacks (ISBN: 0192833286)

GRADE SEVEN – SILVER MEDAL

No Bed for Bacon by Caryl Brahms & S J Simon, Black Swan
    (ISBN: 0552998559)
Year of Wonders by Geraldine Brooks, Fourth Estate (ISBN: 184115458X)
Girl with a Pearl Earring by Tracy Chevalier, HarperCollins
    (ISBN: 0006513204)
The House by the Dvina by Eugenie Fraser, Corgi Adult (ISBN:
    0552128333)
The Glass Palace by Amitav Ghosh, HarperCollins (ISBN: 000651409X)
When We Were Orphans by Kazuo Ishiguro, Faber & Faber
    (ISBN: 057120516X)
Vanity Fair by William Thackeray, Penguin Books (ISBN: 0140620850)
The Time Machine by H G Wells, Phoenix (ISBN: 0460877356)

GRADE EIGHT – GOLD MEDAL

Eva Luna by Isabel Allende, Penguin Books (ISBN: 0140299513)
True History of the Kelly Gang by Peter Carey, Faber & Faber
   (ISBN: 0571209874)
Middlemarch by George Eliot, Oxford Paperbacks (ISBN: 0192834029)
Washington Square by Henry James, Penguin Books (ISBN: 0140432264)
Grace Notes by Bernard MacLaverty, Vintage (ISBN: 0099778017)
A Fine Balance by Rohinton Mistry, Faber & Faber (ISBN: 0571179363)
Here We Are (from *Complete Stories*) by Dorothy Parker, Penguin Books
   (ISBN: 0142437212)
Dracula by Bram Stoker, Penguin Books (ISBN: 014062063X)

Correct at time of publication.

Index of Titles

Index of Authors

Acknowledgements

For permission to reprint the copyright material in the anthology we make grateful acknowledgement to the following authors, publishers and executors:

Adams, Douglas *The Hitchhiker's Guide to the Galaxy* used by permission of Macmillan Publishers Ltd;

Adams, George *The School Play* used by permission of The Orion Publishing Group Ltd;

Alborough, Jez *A Smile* used by permission of Macmillan Children's Books, London UK;

Alcock, Vivien *The Cuckoo Sister* © 1985 Vivien Alcock used by permission of Egmont Books Ltd (UK and Commonwealth) and Houghton Mifflin (US);

Aldis, Dorothy *The Storm* from *All Together* by Dorothy Aldis, © 1925–28, 34, 39, 52, renewed 1953, © 1954–56, 1962 by Dorothy Aldis used by permission of G P Putnam's Sons, a division of Penguin Young Readers Group, A Member of Penguin Group (USA) Inc, all rights reserved;

Allende, Isabel *Eva Luna* translated by Margaret Sayers Peden (Hamish Hamilton, 1989) © Isabel Allende, 1989, English translation © 1991 by Macmillan Publishing Co, reproduced by permission of Penguin Books Ltd;

Almond, David *Skellig* © 1998 reproduced by permission of Hodder & Stroughton Ltd (UK and Commonwealth excl. Canada) and Random House Children's Books, a division of Random House Inc;

Andersen, Hans Christian *The Little Mermaid* from *The Complete Fairy Tales And Stories* by Hans Christian Andersen, translated by Eric Haugaard, © 1974 Eric Haugaard used by permission of Doubleday, a division of Random House Inc;

Angelou, Maya *Still I Rise* used by permission of Time Warner Books UK (UK and Commonwealth) and Random House Inc (US etc);

Armitage, Simon *About His Person* from *Kid* by Simon Armitage used by permission of Faber & Faber;

Armstrong, Martin *Mrs Reece Laughs*, © Martin Armstrong 1921 used by permission of PFD on behalf of the Estate of Martin Armstrong;

Auden, W H *If I Could Tell You* used by permission of Faber & Faber (world excl. US) and Random House Inc (US);

Barker, George *The Great Gales Rage in the Trees* from *Six of the Best* by George Barker used by permission of Faber & Faber;

Bawden, Nina *The Peppermint Pig* used by permission of Curtis Brown on behalf of Nina Bawden, © Nina Bawden 1975;

Belloc, Hilaire *Tarantella* used by permission of PFD on behalf of the Estate of Hilaire Belloc © 1970, the Estate of Hilaire Belloc;

Bloom, Valerie *Water Everywhere* used by permission of The Orion Publishing Group Ltd;

Bodecker, N M *Hippopotamus* from *Snowman Sniffles* by N M Bodecker used by permission of Faber & Faber;

Brahms, Caryl; Simon, S J *No Bed for Bacon* published by Black Swan, used by permission of Transworld Publishers, a division of The Random House Group Ltd;

Brock, Edwin *Song of the Battery Hen* from *Song of the Battery Hen* published by Secker and Warburg used by permission of David Higham Associates;

Brooks, Geraldine *Year of Wonders* used by permission of HarperCollins Publishers Ltd (UK and Commonwealth excl. Canada and Europe) and Viking Penguin, a division of Penguin Group (USA) Inc. (US etc);

Brown, Christy *Old Lady* unable to trace © holder;

Burnside, John *Penitence* from *The Light Trap* published by Jonathan Cape, used by permission of The Random House Group Ltd;

Carey, Peter *True History of the Kelly Gang* © 2000 by Peter Carey, used by permission of Faber & Faber (UK and Commonwealth excl. Canada and Australia), Alfred A Knopf, a division of Random House Inc (US), Random House Canada (Canada), and University of Queensland Press (Australia);

Causley, Charles *My Mother Saw a Dancing Bear* from *Collected Poems for Children* published by Macmillan used by permission of David Higham Associates;

Chevalier, Tracy *Girl with a Pearl Earring* used by permission of HarperCollins Publishers Ltd (world excl. Canada, US and Philippines) and Plume, an imprint of Penguin Group (USA) Inc. (US etc);

Chisholm, Alison *Water Music* used by permission of the author;

Clark, Leonard *House* used by permission of the Literary Executor of Leonard Clark;

Coatsworth, Elizabeth *Calling in the Cat* unable to trace © holder;

Coldwell, John *I Think my Teacher is a Cowboy* used by permission of Macmillan Children's Books, London, UK;

Collett, Andrew *An Alien Education* used by permission of the author (website: www.wackyverse.com);

Cook, Stanley *Chips* used by permission of the estate of Stanley Cook;

Cooper, Susan *King of Shadows* used by permission of the author (US) and The Random House Group Ltd (world excl. US);

Cope, Wendy *Tich Miller* from *Making Cocoa for Kingsley Amis* by Wendy Cope used by permission of Faber & Faber;

Corbett, Pie *Wind Poem* used by permission of Macmillan Children's Books, London, UK;

Crebbin, June *My Grannies* used by permission of the author;

Crompton, Richmal *William Again* used by permission of Macmillan Children's Books;

Crossley-Holland, Kevin *Arthur: At The Crossing-Places* used by permission of Orion Children's Books;

Cummings, E E *Hist Whist* is reprinted from *Complete Poems* 1904–1962 by E E Cummings, edited by George J. Firmage used by permission of W W Norton & Co. Copyright © 1991 by the Trustees for the E E Cummings Trust and George J Firmage;

de la Mare, Walter *Paint* used by permission of the Literary Trustees of Walter de la Mare and the Society of Authors as their representative;

Dixon, Peter *Marmalade* used by permission of Macmillan Children's Books, London, UK;

Doherty, Berlie *Daydreams* from *The Forsaken Merman* reproduced by permission of Hodder & Stroughton Ltd;

du Maurier, Daphne *Rebecca* reproduced by permission of Curtis Brown Ltd, London on behalf of the Chichester Partnership © Daphne du Maurier 1938;

Duffy, Carol Ann *Deportation* from *Selling Manhattan* by Carol Ann Duffy published by Anvil Press Poetry in 1987;

Eddershaw, Chris *Wolf* used by permission of the author;

Edwards, Richard *Monster* used by permission of James Clarke & Co Ltd;

Eliot, T S *La Figlia Che Piange* used by permission of Faber & Faber (world excl. US) and Harcourt Inc (US);

Fanthorpe, U A *Titania to Bottom* from *Neck Verse* © U A Fanthorpe 1992 used by permission of Peterloo Poets;

Horowitz, Anthony *Stormbreaker* © 2000 reproduced by permission of Walker Books Ltd;

Howker, Janni *The Nature of the Beast* © 1985 Janni Howker, used by permission of Walker Books;

Hughes, Ted *The New Foal* used by permission of Faber & Faber (world excl. US) and Farrar, Straus and Giroux (US);

Ibbotson, Eva *Journey to the River Sea* used by permission of Macmillan Children's Books;

Ishiguro, Kazuo *When We Were Orphans* used by permission of Faber & Faber;

James, Richard *Buried Treasure* unable to trace © holder;

Jennings, Elizabeth *Friends* from *Collected Poems* published by Carcanet used by permission of David Higham Associates;

Jones, Terry *The Lady and the Squire* © Terry Jones 2000, reproduced by permission of Chrysalis Children's Books, an imprint of Chrysalis Books Group Plc;

Juhász, Ferenc (translated by David Wevill) *Birth of a Foal* used by permission of the translator;

Juster, Norton *The Phantom Tollbooth* reproduced by permission of HarperCollins Publishers Ltd;

Katz, Bobbi *Cat Kisses* © 1974 by Bobbi Katz, renewed 1997 @aol.com, used with permission;

Kell, Richard *Pigeons* from *Differences* by Richard Kell published by Chatto & Windus, used by permission of The Random House Group Ltd;

Kitching, John *Sea Shore* used by permission of the author;

Larkin, Philip *At Grass* from *The Less Deceived* used by permission of The Marvell Press, England and Australia;

Lee, Carol Ann *Roses from the Earth: The Biography of Anne Frank* reproduced by permission of Penguin Books Ltd;

Lewis, C S *The Voyage of the Dawn Treader* © C S Lewis Pte. Ltd. 1952 used by permission of The C S Lewis Company Ltd;

Lingard, Joan *Tug of War* published by Puffin, used by permission of David Higham Associates;

MacLaverty, Bernard *Grace Notes* published by Jonathan Cape, used by permission of The Random House Group Ltd (UK and Commonwealth excl. Canada) and the author c/o Rogers, Coleridge & White, London (© Bernard MacLaverty 1997);

Norris, Leslie *Tiger* used by permission of the author;

Parker, Dorothy *Here We Are* from *Complete Stories* by Dorothy Parker, used by permission of Gerald Duckworth & Co Ltd (UK and Commonwealth excl. Canada) and Penguin Group (USA) Inc. (US etc);

Patten, Brian *The River's Story* © Brian Patten 1990 reproduced by permission of the author c/o Rogers, Coleridge & White Ltd., London;

Pearse, Philippa *A Dog So Small* reproduced by permission of Penguin Books Ltd;

Pilling, Christopher *The Meeting Place* used by permission of the author;

Pratchett, Terry *Wyrd Sisters* published by Victor Gollancz, used by permission of The Orion Publishing Group Ltd;

Prelutsky, Jack *I am Falling Off a Mountain* from *The New Kid On The Block* © Jack Prelutsky 1984 used by permission of Egmont Books Ltd;

Prévert, Jacques (translated by Lawrence Ferlinghetti) *To Paint the Portrait of a Bird* © Lawrence Ferlinghetti used by permission of City Lights Books;

Pullman, Philip *The Amber Spyglass* (2001) published by Scholastic, used by permission of the author;

Reeves, James *If Pigs Could Fly* © James Reeves from *The Complete Poems for Children* published by Mammoth;

Rieu, E V *The Paint Box* used by permission of Dominic Rieu;

Rosen, Michael *Busy Day* from *You Tell Me* reproduced by permission of Penguin Books Ltd;

Sachar, Louis *Holes* used by permission of Bloomsbury Publishing Plc;

Sansom, Clive *Elephant Walking* from *Rhythm Rhymes* used by permission of A&C Publishers Ltd;

Sassoon, Siegfried *The Hero* © by kind permission of George Sassoon c/o Barbara Levy Literary Agency (world excl. US) and Penguin Group (USA) Inc (US);

Scannell, Vernon *Grannie* used by permission of the author;

Sensier, Danielle *Experiment* used by permission of the author;

Silverstein, Shel *The Silver Fish* © 1981 Shel Silverstein used by permission of HarperCollins Publishers Ltd;

Stewart, Mary *A Walk in Wolf Wood* reproduced by permission of Hodder & Stroughton Ltd;

Strauss, Gwen *Cinderella* used by permission of the author;

Tessimond, A S J *A Hot Day* unable to trace © holder;

Thomas, Dylan *The Song of the Mischievous Dog* from *Collected Poems* published by Dent used by permission of David Higham Associates (world excl. US) and New Directions Publishing Corp (US);

Thompson, John *The Sunbather* unable to trace © holder;

Thurman, Judith *Going Barefoot* from *Flashlight and Other Poems* © 1976 Judith Thurman, used by permission of Marian Reiner for the author;

Tolkien, J R R *The Fellowship of the Ring* used by permission of HarperCollins Publishers Ltd (world excl. US) and Houghton Mifflin (US);

Trevor, William *Juliet's Story* used by permission of PFD on behalf of William Trevor;

Verne, Jules *Around the World in Eighty Days* used by permission of Oxford University Press;

Weil, Zaro *Shadows* from *Mud, Moon and Me* first published by Orchard Books 1989, division of the Watts Publishing Group Ltd;

Wells, H G *The Time Machine* used by permission of A.P. Watt Ltd on behalf of the Literary Executors of the Estate of H.G. Wells;

Westrup, J M *Flying* unable to trace © holder;

Whitworth, John *Boring* used by permission of the author;

Woolf, Virginia *Flush* used by permission of the Society of Authors on behalf of the Estate of Virginia Woolf (world excl. US) and Harcourt Inc (US);

Wright, Kit *The Magic Box* used by permission of Macmillan Publishers Ltd;

Yeats, W B *The Cat and the Moon* from *The Complete Poems of W B Yeats* used by permission of A P Watt on behalf of Michael B Yeats;

Zephaniah, Benjamin *Face* used by permission of Bloomsbury Publishing Ltd.